If I Only Had...

Wrapping Yourself in God's Truth During Storms of Insecurity

LISA BURKHARDT WORLEY & CATHERINE WEISKOPF

Dedication

To my husband, Jeff, for his loving support of my ministry
and writing pursuits. Thank you for your patience.
—Lisa Burkhardt Worley

To my husband, Arthur, who gave me the support,
love, and time to pursue my dreams.
—Catherine Weiskopf

Table of Contents

Preface

The Root of Greatness

HAVE YOU EVER BEEN insecure about accomplishing something God called you to do? Well, relax; you're in good and holy company. Many of the great personalities of the Bible demonstrated extreme insecurity when God placed a call on their lives. Moses is a prime example.

Imagine Moses, a murderer who has found peace and anonymity in a distant land, getting the call. Just as he's relaxing into his life with a wife, children, and a shepherding job, his world takes a dramatic turn. He spots the flames shooting out of the bush, and God utters the words Moses doesn't want to hear in Exodus 3:9–10: "And now the cry of the Israelites has reached me, and I have seen the way the Egyptians are oppressing them. So now, go. I am sending you to Pharaoh to bring my people the Israelites out of Egypt."

Moses begins to mumble and stutter out numerous excuses as to why he can't accomplish such a task, starting in Exodus 3:11: "Who am I, that I should go to Pharaoh and bring the Israelites out of Egypt?"

Many of his excuses, rooted in insecurity, are the same ones you and I use in our own walk with God. How often do we respond with those same words? *Who am I? I don't do anything well. I will just mess it up.*

Throughout my life, I've always related to Moses. When God asked me to take on various tasks, I sounded like my ancient friend. *Who am I? Why would God want to use me?*

This book is based on a series of Bible study lectures God called me to present in the context of the women's ministry of my local church. I remember when the Lord first prompted me to write the material. Like Moses, my first thought was, *Who am I to take this project on?* followed shortly by other excuses: *I don't have enough time. I don't think people will attend the study. I don't have enough to say.* Worried that it was too great a job, I asked another speaker to help me write and present the lectures. After praying about it, she said, "I can help you, but I believe you're the one who is supposed to do it." Still uncertain about my calling and ability, I left my fate in the hands of our Bible study leaders. They were three strong, opinionated women, and I knew they would all be brutally honest about their feelings. I asked God to make their decision unanimous if I was to write the teaching material.

All three said the same thing. "Lisa, you are supposed to do it."

A bit weak in the knees, I began to write a series of lectures on overcoming insecurity. I wondered whether Moses felt this same trepidation when he set off with his sheep herding staff for Egypt. Then I remembered the rest of Moses' story. After God called Moses, he did not leave him stranded in the wilderness. No, he never left his side, guiding him every day until Moses' call was completed. Writing the lectures was the same. God provided the messages, one after the other. At the completion of the study, several attendees asked whether anything else could be done with the material so other women could benefit from it. I made the decision to write this book, and thanks to my co-author, Catherine Weiskopf, the lectures were transformed into *If I Only Had...*

Yes, Moses and I have much in common. We both had our list

of excuses springing from insecurity. Moses' list continued with, *I don't have enough knowledge to do this; I don't have the skills*; and toward the end, he tells God, *Find someone else!*

But God had answers for all of Moses' insecurities and rationalizations, and eventually, the pillar of faith said yes to the call of God; he did a great work for which he will forever be remembered. Because Moses was God's choice, he equipped him to manage a mighty project for him. To demonstrate God's supernatural power, the Lord transformed Moses' staff into a snake, and one day, Moses would use the staff to part the Red Sea as the Israelites escaped captivity.

God also does not leave us empty handed as he calls us out of our safe lives to bold lives for him. While he doesn't provide us with a knotted staff, he does bestow a pillar of strength in the gift of his truth.

When we go out into extreme weather, a scarf protects our lungs. For the winter cold, a thick scarf keeps chilly air at bay. People who live in the Middle East and experience sand storms also use scarves to keep sand from blowing into their nostrils and mouth. Like a person heading out into bad weather, do you take enough time in your day to wrap yourself in God's truth?

Throughout this book, look for powerful **scarves of truth** based on Scripture to protect yourself as you make your escape from the pounding storms of insecurity.

Time and time again, the theme repeats itself. Instead of God's scarf of truth, we wrap ourselves in deception. We follow our emotions and get pulled every which way believing something or someone else will make us secure. Instead, unwrap the slander, throw it in the laundry, and replace it with God's scarves of truth.

Just as Moses lifted up his shortcomings to God, we must do the same. This book also provides you with **prayer gloves** to slip into after each chapter as you offer your insecurities to God. Ephesians 6:18 encourages us to "pray in the Spirit on all occasions with all kinds of prayers and requests." Being real, needy, and urging about our insecurities is no exception. Wesley said we should persevere in prayer until "we come to the end of this holy exercise."

Praying is talking to God directly about our needs. The gloves of prayer in each chapter acknowledge our intent to come to the Master Carpenter first for the fixing of our insecurity issues. God wants to protect us from the storms of insecurity. God wants us to toss aside the excuses and be willing to allow him to heal us.

Insecurity was at the root of Moses' greatness, and God can use our insecurity, as well, to achieve greatness for him. When we feel God tapping us on the shoulder, he's got a job for us, and we can count on him to equip us.

Through the pages of this book, we will work through some of the "if onlys" that prevent us from being all God has called us to be.

Lisa Burkhardt Worley

One

If I Only Had . . .
More Confidence

FROM THE DAY WE are born until the day we die, external forces chisel away at our confidence, and our "if onlys" begin. Our external forces could be family members, friends, tragic circumstances, or a gawky childhood. A hammer of harsh words here, a pounding of neglect there, and pretty soon we feel more like a demolition site than a child of God. These holes of insecurities create cracks in our lives and threaten to affect how we respond to what life tosses us.

Yes, we seemed doomed to deal with the same issues over and over again and to suffer from the same lifelong insecurities.

But there is hope for restoration. There is someone who can fix our holes and shore up our cracks—the Great Carpenter.

My "if onlys" took root two months before I was born, on a typically warm Sunday afternoon at the Brackenridge Park Polo Fields in San Antonio, Texas. My father, Dr. William L. Burkhardt, who liked to be called "Bill," was a successful physician who loved to play competitive polo on the weekends. The usual smallish crowd, made up mostly of the players' family members, attended the match. My mother, in full bloom with her pregnancy, and my fourteen-year-old half-sister were both on hand to cheer my father on, but with the competition in full swing, a hush fell over the spectators. They watched in disbelief as my father keeled over and fell off his horse. There was a great deal of confusion at first. No one knew what happened to my dad until paramedics figured out it was his heart.

My father didn't survive the trip to the hospital, dying swiftly from a massive heart attack at age thirty-nine. My mother's "if onlys" started that day. *If only my husband had not died, I would not be reliant on alcohol and prescription drugs to get through the day. If only he'd had life insurance, I would not be destitute. If only Bill had lived, I could be stronger for my daughter.*

My father's death was one of those external factors no one could control, but it set the stage for my lifelong struggle with fear of abandonment and a propensity to overachieve.

What external forces have shaped your life?

Our insecurity roots run deep. We are born into and grow up in an environment where repeated messages give us a picture of who we are and how the world works. This programming, as it is often called, is powerful and difficult to overcome. To change it, we need to undergo a bit of remodeling.

I am reminded of an episode of *This Old House* in which remodelers rewired a historical home. Old electrical lines are fire hazards. Similarly, old messages we tell ourselves are dangerous to our lives. We must take the old messages of insecurity and replace them with new messages based on God's truth. We must rewire our old house.

One holy rewiring in the Bible involved Gideon. The story begins in Judges 6:11–14:

> The angel of the Lord came and sat down under the oak in Ophrah that belonged to Joash the Abiezrite, where his son Gideon was threshing wheat in a winepress to keep it from the Midianites. When the angel of the Lord appeared to Gideon, he said, "The Lord is with you, mighty warrior."

"Pardon me, my lord," Gideon replied, "but if the LORD is with us, why has all this happened to us? Where are all his wonders that our ancestors told us about when they said, 'Did not the LORD bring us up out of Egypt?' But now the LORD has abandoned us and given us into the hand of Midian."

The LORD turned to him and said, "Go in the strength you have and save Israel out of Midian's hand. Am I not sending you?"

Now listen to this carefully, because here's the insecurity and lack of confidence: "'Pardon me, my lord,' Gideon replied, 'but how can I save Israel? My clan is the weakest in Manasseh, and I am the least in my family.'" (verse 15)

Why do you think Gideon believed he was the "least?" Most likely he was only repeating the messages he received over the years from his family members and extended clan. Was he a little guy? Was he picked on? Gideon accepted what people told him and carried this negative messaging into adulthood. In contrast, remember how the Lord addressed Gideon. He called him "mighty warrior."

Scarf of Truth:
God knows our potential, even if we don't.

I remember the first time I spoke with well-known writer, Max Lucado, in San Antonio. I had worked with his literary agent for a short stretch, trying to get a children's book published. At the time, I was on-air at a local San Antonio television station, and Max probably knew me from that, but when I introduced myself, he said, "Oh, I know you; you're Lisa Burkhardt, the children's book writer."

He was a successful Christian author who believed in my potential as a writer. God also knows our capabilities, even if we don't, and he wants us to hang out in the land of the possible. As Isaiah 64:8 reminds us, "Yet you, LORD, are our Father. We are the clay, you are the potter; we are all the work of your hand."

Do you feel like a lump of clay? Remember, God already sees you as a finished work of art.

Scarf of Truth:
The Lord is with us, even when we lack confidence.

In Judges 6:16–18, God reassures Gideon in the midst of his insecurity: "The LORD answered, 'I will be with you, and you will strike down all the Midianites, leaving none alive.'"

Gideon shows his insecurity again in his response to God's directive. He replies, "'If now I have found favor in your eyes, give me a sign that it is really you talking to me. Please do not go away until I come back and bring my offering and set it before you.'"

The Lord obliges and chills for a while until Gideon returns.

I am like Gideon when I receive what I perceive as a message from God. I want to make sure he's talking to me. It takes three similar holy communiqués before I am confident it's God's direction. I don't fault Gideon for asking his Maker for a sign. Remember, he was coming into this from a vulnerable position, a lifelong history of insecurity. He thought he was the least in his family. He was convinced his clan was the weakest. He was probably thinking, *Why would God want someone like me to do that?*

Isn't this what many of us say when God calls us to accomplish something out of the ordinary? *I am not good enough to do that. I am not equipped. Surely there is someone more suitable for the job.*

If we let the lack of confidence hold our attention, we can miss God's call. Many people let insecurity stop them from living their God assigned adventure. Deanie almost missed out on God's call on her life because of her lack of confidence.

Deanie remembered sitting in her front yard as an elementary school child, cozying up to the invisible boundary separating her yard from her neighbor's. She wasn't supposed to cross the line, invite others over, or venture into the homes of friends. There were rarely visitors at her house because her parents were painfully shy. "Growing up there was always the sense we were separate from everybody," she said about her childhood.

Deanie married during college, and for the next fifteen years, her identity came from taking care of her husband and children. She immersed herself in being a mom. She loved on her children, volunteered for countless jobs, and always had a group to lead.

When she and her family moved to North Texas in the early 1990s, her active life changed. "The neighbors all worked. I didn't have the PTA to get involved in. I didn't have any outlet." Lonely and depressed, she went to a counselor who asked her the simple question, "What do you love to do?" Deanie couldn't answer the question initially but eventually realized her great passions in life were theology and bringing urban and suburban churches together.

When Deanie was forty-six years old, God called her into ministry and she stood on the edge of a precipice. "This was my last chance," she said. Behind her was her old life, and she knew it was killing her. Doubts raced through her mind as she thought of taking the big leap: "Is it too late? What skills do I have? Can I possibly do this?"

"For me, it was life-or-death emotionally," she said. "So I broke our biggest family rule and borrowed money to sign up for seminary." When she paid her fees and walked out, she looked around and wondered what she was doing. "I'd been hanging on and waiting all my life, but at that moment I broke out."

Unfortunately, the self-doubt didn't go away just by taking the first step. Her hands shook during her first test as she hoped twenty years out of school hadn't been too long.

At the end of her first year at seminary, Deanie worried about the next big leap of getting a job when she graduated. She had volunteered and raised a family, but never worked outside the home, which caused her to wonder who would hire her. She felt she was trained for nothing. Because of this, she scheduled an appointment to meet with the district superintendent of her church.

Their meeting started with formalities, and then dramatically took a turn. When the superintendent asked Deanie about preaching, she answered that she didn't want to preach.

"Then what do you want to do?" he asked.

"I didn't come to talk about what I really want to do, but since you asked, I'll tell you," she said. "I really want to connect urban and suburban churches."

Her passion for her calling spilled out. As she talked, his eyes widened, and he was riveted. She later learned it was the superintendent's passion, also. She left his office with a job, a direction, and a new sense of God's involvement in her life. "It was stunning how it all fell into place so quickly," Deanie said. She had no confidence, but God was with her and provided the opportunity she needed to fulfill her calling.

Like Deanie, Gideon lacked confidence and was apprehensive, but he worked through his fear. He gathered up all the items for the offering he promised God, and after he arranged it just right, fire flared from a rock, consuming the meat and the bread. That's when Gideon realized he had been up close and personal with God and had seen the angel of the Lord face-to-face. The Lord knew Gideon was overwhelmed, so he says to him in Judges 6:23-24: "'Peace! Do not be afraid. You are not going to die.' So Gideon built an altar to the Lord there and called it The Lord is Peace."

We all need peace, don't we?

Now that God had Gideon's attention, he asked him to tear down his father's altar to Baal (a false god) and replace it with a proper altar of reverence to God. Gideon did as God requested, but didn't want an audience. Because he was afraid of the men in the town, the still-undercover warrior put on his most inconspicuous robe and snuck out in the middle of the night with ten of his servants to do some altar-smashing. Having a God encounter didn't mean he was healed of his self-doubt. Insecurity had deep roots in Gideon's life, just as it does in ours.

Scarf of Truth:
It may take many encounters with God to overcome insecurity.

Growing up plump, with short blond hair and thick brown glasses, my beauty wasn't the topic of conversation at the lunch table. I hated my looks so much I cut my face out of my sixth-grade class picture, but at some point in my adolescent journey, I believed I was attractive enough to pursue a television sportscasting career. Working in the public eye didn't remove the insecurity about my looks. I complained about my appearance while having lunch with a friend, but she reminded me they don't put ugly people on television. Like Gideon, it took many repeat messages before I believed I wasn't that homely sixth-grader anymore. It may also take you many encounters with God to overcome insecurity.

We are not a one-shot, got-it-the-first-time people. We think we've learned, but we constantly fall back into the same old ways of viewing ourselves. Each time we feel insecure, we live on the edge of danger because we often reach for a quick fix to deal with the uneasy feeling.

The Israelites did the same thing in 1 Samuel 8:5 when they ask Samuel to appoint a king: "You are old, and your sons do not follow your ways; now appoint a king to lead us, such as all the other nations have."

They desired a king because they coveted other nations' monarchies, and they thought they'd feel more secure and protected if they copied their competition. Similarly, we tell ourselves we'll feel more secure if we give something else, like looks or money, lordship over our security. But this strategy never works and does not eliminate the problem. To avoid this dangerous path, we must go to God with our insecurities every time.

Meanwhile, the Israelites' enemies are approaching, and Gideon is shaking in his boots again. He asks God to deliver one more sign that he is the one who is supposed to save Israel. *Are you really sure it's me, God?* In Judges 6:36-37, "Gideon said to God: 'If you will save Israel by my hand as you have promised—look, I will place a wool fleece on the threshing floor. If there is dew only on the fleece and all the ground is dry, then I will know that you will save Israel by my hand, as you said.'"

What's funny here is that Gideon acknowledges God spoke to him, but he still doesn't totally believe it. God patiently took Gideon around the block again after Gideon ordered up one more sign. The next day, the fleece was wet, and the ground was dry. How much more proof did Gideon need?

Scarf of Truth:
In order to overcome insecurity, we must believe what God says about us.

Did you grow up in a dysfunctional family life and now can't seem to get past it? You need to believe that God is your Father. God provides the recipe for becoming his children in John 1:12: "Yet to all who receive him, to those who believed in his name, he gave the right to become children of God."

Do you think you are not pretty enough? You are exactly the way God created you to be. Jeremiah 1:5 tells us: "Before I formed you in the womb I knew you, before you were born I set you apart."

Do you feel you're not good at anything and have no gifts to be used in God's kingdom? Trust Ephesians 2:10: "For we are God's handiwork, created in Christ Jesus to do good works, which God prepared in advance for us to do."

You have a gift God wants you to use. If you don't know what it is, ask him to reveal it to you. Many of us acknowledge the Bible is the inspired Word of God. Yet much like the insecure Gideon, we don't always believe the promises of God's words.

After some Holy repetition, Gideon was finally convinced. God worked through him in an extraordinary way to subdue the

Midianites. Gideon gathered an army of 22,000 men, but God whittled that number down to 300 so he would receive the glory for the victory. When Gideon and the 300 strong arrived at the Midianites' camp, they held torches in their left hands, blew their trumpets, and smashed the empty jars they carried. Then they shouted: "A sword for the Lord and for Gideon!"

Scarf of Truth:
God doesn't always fight our battles in the way we imagine he will.

It's a bizarre way to fight, but . . . unbelievably, the Midianites were rattled by the Israelites' actions and ran, turning on each other with their swords. Gideon and his troops captured and killed the leaders of the Midianites. For the rest of Gideon's life, forty years, there was peace in the land. Amazing! Gideon's self-confidence level was no longer short-circuited. God rewired an insecure man from the "weakest" clan into a mighty warrior and hero.

Whatever battle you are in right now, God, the Master Electrician, may not connect the wires exactly the way you imagine. Since God is a creative God who loves surprises, he rarely follows our design or direction. Wouldn't it be boring if God were predictable?

An elegant woman named Karen remembered how a few words from her husband shattered her world before God began putting the pieces of her broken life back together.

Her husband, Mike, had just returned home from a trip and lay across their bed. "I've fallen in love with another woman," he said, "and I'll be leaving next week."

Nausea raced through Karen's body as she stood frozen with disbelief. "I felt it was all a bad dream and I would wake up soon," Karen said. "I had many questions and needed answers. Of course, I never got them."

Karen prayed Mike would return, and three weeks later, he did ask to come back. "I agreed to let him come home because I didn't want our family broken up, and I loved him very much. We both agreed to try and work things out. The next two years were difficult because Mike traveled all week, but I knew I had to trust my husband if I wanted our marriage to survive."

About the time she felt secure in their marriage, the same nightmare crushed her heart again. This time Mike was moving to East Texas, where his new lover lived. Karen realized her marriage was over and filed for divorce after much prayer. "Again," she said, "I thought my world had ended. I had always been someone's wife and mother, with no identity of my own. I knew I could not continue to feel worthless and deceived."

Karen began attending a separated/divorced support group at her church. There she realized that many others faced even greater adversity. "Helping others through their grief and tragedy helped me." During this time, Karen met her second husband, to whom she has been married for over fourteen years.

"He is a wonderful, kind, and loving man. I learned that God never promised to keep us from trials and difficulties, but God promises to get us through them," Karen said.

We have our own ideas about how things should go, but God's thoughts are not our thoughts. His ways are not our ways. He wants us to have no doubt he is the reason the battle is won.

There was no doubt God was responsible for Gideon's victory. In an excerpt from *Matthew Henry's Bible Commentary*, it has this to say about Gideon:

> While God calls Gideon valiant, he makes him so. God delights to advance the humble. Gideon desires to have his faith confirmed. Now, under the influences of the Spirit, we are not to expect signs before our eyes such as Gideon here desired, but must earnestly pray to God, that if we have found grace in his sight, he would show us a sign in our heart, by the powerful working of his Spirit there.

Gideon worked through his insecurity, probably from his child-hood, to accomplish a great task for God. His story has been an inspiration for many, including two men from Wisconsin who met on a business trip in the fall of 1898. John H. Nicholson and Samuel E. Hill checked into the Central Hotel in Boscobel, Wisconsin, think-ing they would have separate rooms, but the hotel was extremely crowded, so the two ended up sharing a room. That night, while they were getting to know each other, they discovered they were both Christians, so they joined together for an evening devotion and prayer.

Nicholson and Hill's meeting prompted an idea to form an association to band Christian commercial travelers together for service to the Lord. When they were coming up with a name for their group, they immediately agreed they would be called Gideons, based on the sixth and seventh chapters of Judges.

Just like Gideon, they had a big undertaking ahead of them which they would be able to accomplish only through God's power and direction. In the early years of the association, the men decided they could be the most effective witnesses in hotels by placing a Bible in every bedroom of each hotel. That plan was adopted in 1908. One hundred years have passed since The Gideons placed the first Bible in a hotel room in Montana.

Today, Gideons are organized in more than 190 countries around the world. The Bibles and New Testaments are printed in more than ninety languages, with 1.6 billion Bibles and New Testaments placed in the hotels. 1.6 billion! I cried when I read that number, and was so impressed that it all started with two ordinary men, probably with their own insecurities, who shared the Word and prayed together in a hotel room. It's incredible, and so interest-ing they named themselves after an insecure hero named Gideon who finally believed what God had to say to him.

I know many of us still fight the negative messages we received during childhood, but if you've accepted Christ, you are a new creation, and the Lord wants you to be secure in Him. We have to let go of our old selves and trust God's blueprint for our lives. Call it a battle. Call it holy rewiring. Call it whatever you want, but God needs to do some remodeling in us. All our internal baggage from the past is rubbish compared to the assurances of God.

One of my favorite verses is Joel 2:25. It promises us that God will repay us for the years the locusts have eaten. I don't know about you, but there were a lot of "if only" locusts gnawing away at me in my early years, but in order to overcome, I finally had to trust God like Gideon did.

Are you ready to fight back against the obstacles that prevent you from being secure? Do you desire to discard all your "if onlys?" Know you can trust God with your battle, and stand firm on his promises as he wages war against the insecurity within you. So let's forge ahead together on that journey to claim victory in our lives. The Lord is with you, mighty warrior princess. The Lord is with you!

Gloves of Prayer: *Lord, please begin a holy rewiring in me, and help me overcome a past that destroys my confidence. Give me your eyes, dear God, to see myself as you see me, not as I feel about myself. Show me how to believe I am your handiwork, created in Christ Jesus to do good works for you. Give me your vision for my life, and strengthen me to be a great warrior of the faith. In Jesus' name, AMEN.*

Discussion Questions:
If I Only Had . . . More Confidence

1. From the day we are born until the day we die, external forces chisel away at our confidence, and our "if onlys" begin. What people or experiences in your life have caused you to feel insecure? What external forces have shaped your life? Like Gideon, what messages have you heard over and over again until they have become truth to you?

2. Like rewiring an old house, we must take old messages of insecurity and replace them with new messages based on God's truth. What messages of God's truth can you use to replace the lies of insecurity that fill your head?

3 Gideon felt unworthy of leading the Israeli army to victory. Like Gideon, have you ever felt God calling you to do something and doubted the call and your worthiness? Has God confirmed that calling?

4. When God called Gideon, Gideon reacted the following three ways:

   "But Lord, how can I . . .",
   "If I have found favor send me a sign.",
   He did what the Lord told him, but he did it at night, when no one was watching.

   What interaction between Gideon and God do you most identify with?

5. The Israelites asked for a king when they were feeling insecure. What shortcuts or temporary fixes do you tend to gravitate toward when you are feeling insecure?

6. God wants us to hang out in the land of the possible. How can you make changes in your life so you will be more pliable clay in the Potter's hands?

7. Like Max Lucado calling Lisa the children's book writer, imagine God introducing you to someone. How might he describe you?

8. God doesn't always fight our battles the way we imagine he will. Has God healed you from some of your insecurities in ways you never expected? If so, how?

9. The Bible is full of promises from God about who you are and your importance. You may read the Bible and even study it, but do you believe what the Word of God says about you? What do you readily believe, and what do you have trouble believing?

10. Gideon Bibles are placed in hotels around the world and have inspired many people to accept Christ. Do you think John Nicholson and Samuel Hill ever imagined they would influence millions of people? What do you think God could accomplish through you if you allowed him to use your life?

Two

If I Only Had . . .
Healthy Thoughts

BEN, THE SON OF a friend, burst in the door after school one day, yelling. "It's so unfair, Mom. Coach took me off the relay team." Ben explained how his name had been crossed off each relay event and replaced by another runner. Ben's mood quickly changed from anger to doubt as he sought a reason for this change.

"Did I mess up in the race last week?" he asked.

"No, you did great," his mother said.

"I was awful, and that's why he took me off the team."

"Ben, if anyone on your team hadn't done a fabulous job you wouldn't have finished first."

It was true. Each handoff had been perfect, and each sprinter had passed at least one runner.

"Maybe he took you out because there is too much conflict with pole-vault," she said. To run each relay-race, Ben had to leave the pole-vault competition, race, and then return to pole-vault when the race was finished.

Ben oscillated back and forth between upset and anger for awhile. It was finally resolved the day of the track meet.

The coach decided to take Ben out of the running events

because he was privy to information unknown to Ben and his mom. At the location for the track meet, pole-vaulting and running two races would be impossible. The pole-vault area was blocks away from the track. Ben was upset for nothing. Like Ben, how often are our unhealthy thoughts pointless? How often do we, grasping for a reason, imagine something that isn't true and take ourselves on an emotional roller-coaster?

What if there were a way to measure these unhealthy roller-coaster thoughts? Imagine if someone invented a thought thermometer—an instrument to monitor our thoughts and alert us when they wandered into the danger zone. Put it in your ear, press a button, and your thoughts would register somewhere between the boiling point and absolute zero. It would be like a mood ring that actually works. Would your thoughts ever have a healthy temperature of 98.6? Are you usually too hot or too cold? We know negative thinking can make us sick, but we still spend too much time debilitated by its infection.

Fortunately, we know we are not alone. Jonah was a man whose thought temperature registered two lines short of the boiling point. Let's start with his assignment from God in Jonah 1:1-2: "The word of the LORD came to Jonah son of Amittai: 'Go to the great city of Nineveh and preach against it, because its wickedness has come up before me.'"

God wasn't sending Jonah on a vacation to the Bahamas. Nineveh was the home of one of the Israelites' archenemies, the Assyrians, who were known for their gruesome torture tactics. I can almost hear Jonah's response.

Are you kidding, God? I'm very fond of my hands and feet, and how am I going to be your prophet if they make my tongue a keepsake? (The Assyrians were the ones who destroyed the Northern Kingdom of Israel in 734 B.C. That was just over fifty years after the book of Jonah was written.)

Telling Jonah to preach to the Assyrians would be like God

asking you to go preach about Jesus to a terrorist group. Are you anxious to volunteer?

Jonah didn't like the Assyrians, and he didn't want to tell them to repent, because in his mind, they were *bad* people. Do you see Jonah's thought temperature rising? His temperature rose so high it caused his feet to run the opposite direction, away from God's call. Frankly, he didn't understand what God was thinking.

The same applies to us. We often don't understand God's mind map for our life? Whether it is about our looks or our husbands, our children or our friends, we must first recognize our thoughts are not God's.

Scarf of Truth:
Our thoughts and God's thoughts do not always sync up.

Stay with me on this. If God's thinking and your thinking do not line up, whose thinking needs changing? One reason we read the Bible is so God can reveal to us how he wants us to look at things.

In Matthew 6:34, Scripture tells us, "Therefore do not worry about tomorrow, for tomorrow will worry about itself. Each day has enough trouble of its own."

God clearly states that we should not worry, but I challenge you to count all the worried thoughts you have during the course of a day. Not too healthy?

James 1:2–3 says, "Consider it pure joy, my brothers and sisters, whenever you face trials of many kinds, because you know that the testing of your faith produces perseverance." Let's be honest, when we are going through a trial, do we celebrate?

It's not easy or immediate, but immersing ourselves in God's Word will move us from our natural thinking to God's thinking. Reading God's Word becomes learning God's Word. Learning God's Word becomes using God's Word. Using God's Word becomes living God's Word, and that is when we see real changes in our thought temperature.

Back to Jonah. Jonah's cruise to Tarshish became rocky when a violent storm threatened to tear the boat apart. Things like this always happen when you are trying to run away from the Master of the Universe. So Jonah, in an "aha" moment, said to his fellow crew members, *Sorry, guys, but I think this storm is raging because I'm trying to escape from God. If you want to throw me overboard, that may clear up the weather.* Notice that the crew, in deciding whether to save themselves or save Jonah, didn't hesitate to hear the prophet's body go *kerplunk.*

Many times, God gives us a gentle push—or as in Jonah's case, a big shove—to get us back on track. As soon as Jonah's feet hit the waves, the sea grew calm. In most cases, a man overboard without a life vest would be good as dead. The sailors knew that and cried out to the Lord, asking him to spare their lives for taking Jonah's. But we all know that Jonah did not die. God just needed to give Jonah some time to hear his voice. That's why he sent the big fish to swallow up the runaway prophet for three days and three nights. By allowing this to occur, God took away all of Jonah's distractions. It gave God time to work on Jonah's thinking. Jonah went from ship-bound to fish-bound, from running time to thinking time.

At this point, awareness is forming at the edge of Jonah's brain that his thoughts and God's thoughts are not aligned. The temperature on his thought thermometer is creeping down. There is hope for Jonah's condition, after all.

Scarf of Truth:
Sometimes we need to change our surroundings in order to change our thinking.

We hope that when God wants to talk to us, he will employ more subtle tactics. Sometimes, all he wants is for us to take a break from our preoccupation with the world. No e-mails. No phone ringing. No TV. No Facebook. You must be intentional about separating yourself from distractions.

Years ago, I went through something difficult and was in a downward spiral. I went away to a friend's house in the country and spent two entire days praying and immersed in God's Word. God took all the negative thoughts I had built up and turned them around 180 degrees. After changing my surroundings and spending a great deal of one-on-one time with God, I was a new woman.

Changing our surroundings can open us to hearing God's voice, and most of us don't need to stare at fish ribs from the inside to get to this point. We simply need time without a list of household chores calling our name. I'm not talking fifteen minutes alone with God. I am suggesting hours or a full day, submerged in prayer and God's Word, petitioning God for victory in whatever area of insecurity you struggle with. Ask God to help you believe his promises to you. Ask him to adjust your thought temperature to be more like his.

Jonah found the truth while sitting in the belly of the big fish. He had uninterrupted thinking time, and gradually his unhappiness with his Creator transformed into gratitude. Here's what he had to say in Jonah 2:1–7:

> From inside the fish Jonah prayed to the LORD his God. He said: "In my distress I called to the LORD, and he answered me. From deep in the realm of the dead, I called for help, and you listened to my cry. You hurled me into the depths, into the very heart of the seas, and the currents swirled about me; all your waves and breakers swept over me. (Have you ever felt this way, like you're drowning?) I said, 'I have been banished from your sight; yet I will look again toward your holy temple.' The engulfing waters threatened me. The deep surrounded me; seaweed was wrapped around my head. To the roots of the mountains I sank down; the earth beneath barred me in forever. But you, LORD my God, brought my life up from the pit.

When my life was ebbing away, I remembered you, LORD, and my prayer rose to you, to your holy temple."

It's amazing how living in the belly of the fish for three days can transform your thinking. Jonah went from running from God's view to seeing God's truth for his life.

Scarf of Truth:
When we finally acknowledge God's truths about our lives, he will rescue us from negative thoughts and insecurity.

According to Joyce Meyer in her book, *Power Thoughts,* "Being positive does not mean we deny the existence of difficulty; it means we believe God is greater than our difficulties. Believing in God can cause us to win any battle we face."[1] Meyer says we need to train our brain to trust and believe God, and to think positive thoughts that are based on his Word.

There are many rich truths in this passage from Jonah, but let me focus on verses 5–6, because I think it's where we go sometimes with our own personal situations. Jonah said the engulfing waters threatened him, the deep surrounded him, he had seaweed wrapped around his head, he sank down to the roots of the mountains, and the earth beneath him barred him in forever.

Forever?

Do you ever think like Jonah? *This is never going to get better. He is never going to change. I don't think I will ever get over this one.*

Was it forever for Jonah? No, but his thoughts were negative, and his thought temperature was registering hot. Then Jonah praises God when he says: "but you, LORD my God, brought my life up from the pit." Maybe his forever thinking wasn't quite right, after all. Jonah just needed some time away with God in a different environment.

What happens when we are sick with food poisoning or, in this case, mind poisoning? Our body has to get rid of it. At the end of this passage, the big fish, at the Lord's command, vomits Jonah up onto dry land. He is feeling a lot better now, and thinking a lot more clearly, although he smells like fish guts.

In Jonah's case, God gave him another opportunity to go and proclaim his message to the great city of Nineveh, and guess what? Jonah obeyed God and did what he asked him to do.

Scarf of Truth:
God will give us more opportunities to think rightly.

That's one more quality to love about God—he gives us repeated chances to get our thinking right. If we don't get the heavenly text this time, he will resend. Of course, this doesn't mean we should put off our changes, but it does mean he is gracious.

God opened Bridget's eyes to his truth twenty-five years after she had readily accepted the opinions of teenage boys as fact. He gave her another chance to see her childhood experience through his eyes. She clearly remembered one instance of the bullying.

Bridget moaned internally when Mr. Novak's keys jingled as he headed out the classroom door, leaving behind a room full of seventh graders reading in their seats. He was leaving the class-room for the third time that week which meant it was open harass-ment season on the undesirables. Hoping they would choose a different target today, Bridget lowered her eyes and shrunk down in her seat. John, the shortest boy in class, and instigator, turned around in his chair and glared at Bridget. "Beanpole," he sneered.

Bridget's face burned red as the feeling of being worthless flowed throughout her awkward, skinny six-foot-tall frame.

"Bridget plus Danny equals love," Andy said, joining in the put-downs.

Snickers echoed in the room. Bridget wanted to disappear. She scribbled in her notepad pretending she didn't care. But inside their disapproval felt like it was branding her heart with a big "L" for loser.

Bridget then heard the familiar sound of Mr. Novak's keys as he walked toward the classroom.

"Quiet, he's coming," said John.

Bridget took a deep breath. *It was over for today.*

Over the years, Bridget interpreted the torment from these two boys as proof something was wrong with her. Although she heard encouraging words from people around her, the way the boys treated her felt more like the truth.

Years later, when she returned to her hometown, God opened her eyes.

"There was a hill in our flat town in northwest Iowa. As a child, we would ride blocks out of our way not to go up the hill because of its daunting slope. I laughed when I saw the small incline accurately for the first time. Then the light went on. If I had seen the hill so inaccurately, maybe the same was true of how people treated me."

She realized that instead of the boys making fun of her because something was wrong with her, they made fun of her because they envied her height. This God-given insight began the healing of her self-image. Bridget was finally thinking rightly about herself.

So where did Jonah end up? Miraculously, after Jonah preached to the Assyrians, they believed God and repented. I wish I could say there was a "happily ever after" to this story, but the ending didn't quite go that way. Jonah should have skipped all the way back from Nineveh, right? He had broken the negative thought pattern. He had been on the same page with God since his weekend vacation at sea. However, that's not what happened.

After dealing with the situation, he slipped right back into his own negative thoughts, and his thought temperature spiked again. The spiritual high Jonah experienced did not last long.

Scarf of Truth:
We must keep our focus on God to keep the negative thoughts from returning.

After Jonah preached to the Assyrians, he wasn't pleased about his archenemies' repentance. The Assyrians did what God asked them to do, but that made Jonah angry about their transformation, praying in Jonah 4:2–3: "'Isn't this what I said, LORD, when I was still at home? That is what I tried to forestall by fleeing to Tarshish. I knew that you are a gracious and compassionate God, slow to anger and abounding in love, a God who relents from sending calamity. Now, LORD, take away my life, for it is better for me to die than to live.'"

Jonah has a few good days, full of praising God for saving him from a dire situation. "Yes, Lord, I believe your truths. I will do what you tell me to do." But then, after his obedience, he goes right back into the pit, back into the same negative thought patterns about the Assyrians. He revisits his past mindset about what he wants and doesn't want, what he believes is fair and unfair. Does this sound familiar? We have some victory days, then we start dwelling on the bad, and soon, our temperature is getting hotter. How do we stop the cycle? How do we get well?

Here's a suggestion. Try being your own thought thermometer:

Take your thought temperature on a regular basis. Notice especially the hot emotions—anger, anxiety, and jealousy. Do you have negative thoughts in a healthy amount? Do you get stuck on worry, or become angry and upset? When you wake up in the middle of the night, do your thoughts churn so you can't go back to sleep? Ask the Lord to renew your thoughts if they are not of him.

In Psalm 139:23–24, King David, whose thoughts could spiral downward, asked God: "Search me, O God, and know my heart; test me and know my anxious thoughts. See if there is any offensive way in me, and lead me in the way everlasting." The trick is recognizing which thoughts are like viruses and which are like vitamins.

Go to the Great Healer. Remember where real truth comes from and get a prescription from Jesus. He wants us to spend time in his Word so he can shed light on the darkness of our thinking as he says in Psalm 119:105: "Your word is a lamp to my feet and a light to my path."

Let God perform surgery and replace your thoughts with his thoughts. In Philippians 4:8, Paul encourages us, "Finally brothers and sisters, whatever is true, whatever is noble, whatever is right, whatever is pure, whatever is lovely, whatever is admirable—if anything is excellent or praiseworthy—think about such things."

When we have negative thoughts, do we ask ourselves, "Is this right? Is this pure? Is this lovely, admirable, excellent, or praiseworthy?" If we really grasped the truth that God is aware of all of our thoughts, would we attempt to change? Psalm 94:11 reminds us: "The Lord knows all human plans; he knows that they are futile."

The good news is that change is possible through the power of Christ. Romans 12:1–2 speaks to this:

> Therefore, I urge you, brothers and sisters, in view of God's mercy, to offer your bodies as a living sacrifice, holy and pleasing to God—this is your true and proper worship. Do not conform to the pattern of this world, but be transformed by the renewing of your mind. Then you will be able to test and approve what God's will is—his good, pleasing and perfect will. When you renew your mind, the destructive and unhealthy thoughts will be wiped clean.

Did Jonah ever find his way to healthy thinking or did he take another fishy vacation? We will never know. The story ends with Jonah still angry and pouting. Jonah sat down outside Nineveh, made himself a shelter, and God caused a vine to grow up over Jonah to give him shade. The next day, God also provided a worm, which chewed the vine so it withered. Jonah became angry about that, as well—he liked his vine—and again wanted to die. This is the way God leaves it in Jonah 4:9–11:

> But God said to Jonah, "Is it right for you to be angry about the plant?"
>
> "It is," he said. "And I'm so angry I wish I were dead."
>
> But the LORD said, "You have been concerned about this plant, though you did not tend it or make it grow. It sprang up overnight and died overnight. And should I not have concern for the great city of Nineveh, in which there are more than a hundred and twenty thousand people who cannot tell their right hand from their left—and also many animals?"

And that is how the book of Jonah ends, abruptly. So many times, when we are in one of those negative thought patterns, we cannot escape from our pity parties long enough to see the bigger picture. Jonah had the problem, and so do we.

Scarf of Truth:
When we take our minds off ourselves and remain focused on God, we are better able to see his bigger picture.

Abby remembered how focused she was on herself in junior high and how miserable it made her. One day, while attending bell choir and confirmation at church, she heard something painful as she approached her group of friends.

"Wasn't that fun," Jeanne said.

"Jane's parties are the best," Cindy said.

A lump formed in Abby's throat as she realized she hadn't been invited to her best friend's birthday party.

Quiet and sullen during bell choir and confirmation, she kept to herself. She wasn't able to cry until she arrived home.

"I couldn't understand why all the girls I hung out with were invited but I was left out," said Abby.

"I spent days crying and talking to my mom about the situation. *Wasn't I good enough? Wasn't I funny enough? What had I done to deserve being left out?*"

Abby's parents were always the life of the party, but having the good-girl image in junior high and high school kept her on the outside of the social circles. "Here I was, the daughter of the life of the party, and I couldn't even get invited to a party."

In adulthood, this "wanting to be invited" still plagued Abby. "December has always been difficult for me," she says. "It's a social time. I saw people going out to their parties while I stayed home." And then people would talk about it. "I was rock-bottom one December," she explains. Everyone around her seemed to be having so much fun. She wondered what was wrong with her and why she hadn't been invited.

During this time, Abby found a new friend. Her new friend was bubbly and had a list of party invitations a mile long. This woman had a ministry at church, and Abby found herself so hooked onto this friend for her security that she sent her a text message she now regrets. "Do you like me enough to hang out with me?" Abby is now embarrassed by what insecurity caused her to do. The remark, the hurt, and the emotions nearly ended a wonderful friendship.

Instead, God began working on her heart. She felt God tell her to stand still, and guard her heart, and he would order her path. So, for three months, this is exactly what she did. She felt like the Israelites between the approaching armies and the Red Sea. How was God going to get her out of this mess of emotions? How was God going to lead her to a more secure place?

The answer came in an unexpected way. Instead of fretting about what she didn't have, God moved her focus to others. Now, she is a woman with a ministry of her own that centers on those in financial need. This ministry has been a godsend to many, but it also ministered to Abby's insecure heart. She gained a glimpse of God's plan for her life and his love for her. She now knows that her ultimate security lies in God.

We have an enemy—Satan. He is a deceiver, and if he renders us ineffective because we believe his whispers, he wins. When we fight back and say, "I don't believe that. It does not line up with God's Word," then God wins. Our fever goes down, the glaze on our eyes melts away, and we can see how this all fits into God's plan. We are commanded in 2 Corinthians 10:5: "We demolish arguments and every pretension that sets itself up against the knowledge of God, and we take captive every thought to make it obedient to Christ."

So when you are stuck in negative thoughts or messages, do you ask yourself whether your thoughts are obedient to Christ? Do they line up with God's Word? Do they prevent you from looking at the big picture? That's what I think God wanted Jonah to assimilate. You are angry about a vine that you didn't have anything to do with, Jonah. I am worried about thousands upon thousands of people. That's the big picture.

I am not saying there are no serious issues in life to be concerned about. But many times, the things that get us down are beyond our control and not important in the overall scheme of life, just like the vine Jonah wanted to die over. I challenge you to pay attention to what you are worried about, and see how many negative thoughts creep into your mind each day. Take them captive. Check your thought thermometer daily, because when your temperature goes back to normal and the glaze comes off your eyes, you will see a world out there that God wants you to reach.

Gloves of Prayer: *Lord, I desperately want to have a healthy thought temperature. As it says in your Word, help me to think about whatever is noble, whatever is right, whatever is pure, whatever is lovely, whatever is admirable—and anything that is* *excellent or praiseworthy. Remind me to take every thought captive to you as I allow you to steer my thoughts from being centered on myself towards thinking about how I can help others and love you. I want to be a bright light for you rather than a dark alley that people avoid. Thank you for lowering my thought temperature. In Jesus' name, AMEN.*

Discussion Questions:
If I Only Had . . . Healthy Thoughts

1. Imagine someone invented a thought thermometer. Would your thought temperature be a healthy 98.6, or would you always be running a fever? If you have a fever, which thoughts are making you ill?

2. Jonah was a man whose thought temperature registered two lines short of the boiling point. "The word of the LORD came to Jonah son of Amittai. 'Go to the great city of Nineveh and preach against it, because its wickedness has come up before me.' But Jonah ran away from the LORD and headed for Tarshish." Have you ever been like Jonah and run the opposite direction when God called you? If so, why?

3. Isaiah 55:8 says, "'For my thoughts are not your thoughts, neither are your ways my ways,' declares the LORD." Describe a time in your life when your thinking and God's thinking were not the same on a problem or issue.

4. Jonah found the truth while sitting in the belly of the big fish reflecting on his life, away from the world. Has God ever allowed you to hang out in the "belly of a whale" or given you time away for reflection? What did he say to you while you were there?

5. Sometimes we need to change our surroundings in order to change our thinking. Have you ever changed your surroundings and come back with a different mindset? Describe a time when you felt sorry for yourself but after helping someone in a worse situation felt a renewed thankfulness for all you have.

6. Jonah said, "To the roots of the mountains I sank down; the earth beneath barred me in forever." Like Jonah, are you an extremist thinker? Do you use the word "forever" or "never" or "always" a lot? For example: *This always happens to me* or *this is never going to change.* Remember a time when you used or thought these words. Was this thinking realistic? How was this thinking destructive?

7. Bridget interpreted the torment from two boys as proof that something was wrong with her. Years later, when she returned to her hometown, God opened her eyes. Describe a time when God has turned your thinking around and opened your eyes to his truth.

8. We must keep our focus on God to keep the negative thoughts from returning. How can you take your negative thoughts and transform them into praise and thankfulness?

9. The scripture 2 Corinthians 10:5 says, "We demolish arguments and every pretension that sets itself up against the knowledge of God, and we take captive every thought to make it obedient to Christ." How can you take your thoughts captive to Christ? What are some practical things you do to keep your focus on God rather than on your negative thoughts?

10. Changing our thoughts begins with awareness. Practical ways of taking your thought temperature include setting a reminder alarm on your phone, posting scriptural reminders around the house, and having an accountability partner. Make a plan to enact ways to take your thought temperature. What are some practical ways you can take your own thought temperature on a regular basis?

Three

If I Only Had . . .
Peace

MY DISDAIN OF HEIGHTS began after a trip to the local amusement park with my aunt, when I was about eight years old. We paid for our tickets and climbed aboard an ominous Ferris wheel. As the wheel ascended and crested, it stopped cold, leaving us hanging and swinging. At first, I thought the operator was trying to scare us, but then I realized something was wrong. We were stuck at the top.

I cried and screamed as we rocked back-and-forth sixty feet off the ground. Below us, men frantically worked, trying to rescue us from the steel monster that held us captive. I clutched the side of my seat as ten minutes creaked by, then fifteen. After twenty long minutes, the old Ferris wheel finally groaned to life.

My piggies were never so happy as that day when they touched ground! Since my "terror at the top" experience, I have never been up in another Ferris wheel, and I hate it when my feet dangle from any kind of elevation.

What were your fears growing up? Did you check under your bed at night as a child? Do you recall waking up after dark, seeing a shadow, and being convinced that a wind-tossed tree was a monster about to do you in? Or did a friend ever hide behind a bush and jump out and frighten you so badly you felt as if your heart would stop? As adults, we may no longer worry about boogiemen, but we still have fears that rob us of peace. Failing at a new job, losing a loved one, kids going down the wrong path, bad health or disease, and death are just a few worries that contribute to our sleepless nights.

At its most basic level, fear is a feeling—a reaction to danger, real or perceived. Real fear seizes you when you walk to your car late at night and someone grabs you from behind. Perceived fear is the knot you get in your stomach when your child is two hours late returning home, and you imagine everything that could have happened. Your body cannot tell the difference between real and perceived fear.

Some fears are natural, immediate, and intense reactions to danger. It is, after all, a part of our fight-or-flight survival mechanism. We see it in the predator-prey dance in the wild. The human race would not have lasted without some trepidation. Your panic injects extra adrenaline into your system, working as a catalyst to spring you into action. If you were ever in real danger, the right kind of distress would be your best friend. The wrong kind of fear is what we must strive to overcome.

Extreme fear can also stem from a physical component, and may be brought on by long-term stress or hormonal changes. Many families have a genetic disposition toward anxiety-based disorders. Jillian started having anxiety attacks during a difficult move from Illinois to Texas. She was fixing up the house, selling it, and getting ready for Christmas, all at the same time. Driving for two days with a pair of dogs, she finally joined her husband in a Texas hotel room—their temporary residence. Jillian was exhausted.

"As soon as I sat down to relax, it was as if something else took over," Jillian said.

The plaid bedspread seemed to tip and spin. She grabbed the bed hoping to steady herself. The room pulsated as she fell face first on the bed.

"I didn't know where I was," Jillian remembered, "or what was happening."

"Help, me!" she yelled to her husband.

"What happened?" he asked as he ran to her side.

"I think I passed out," she said, trying to make some sense of her confusion.

"No, you didn't," he answered, making the assessment based on her lack of a pale face.

Her mind raced. "Then I must be going crazy," she screamed, holding her head. Now full of adrenaline, she imagined herself in horrible circumstances; she was in a mental ward; she was dying; she was having a stroke. Shaking uncontrollably, she grabbed her husband, "I don't think I can take this," she said.

"What do you want to do?"

"Call for help," she said.

Her husband called a hotline, and Jillian talked to a counselor.

"This woman knew what was happening to me and in my mind I did, too. I knew I was going crazy and was just putting off an eventual trip to the psychiatric hospital. Jillian shook all night, terrified, wondering how she was going to survive in this place so far away from all her family and friends. That's when her three-year battle with panic attacks began.

We must acknowledge that paralyzing fear, like the kind Jillian experienced, often comes from our enemy, Satan. The *New King James Version* of 2 Timothy 1:7 says it best: "For God has not given us a spirit of fear, but of power and of love and of a sound mind."

Satan delights when we are too scared to act. It is a common theme among even the giants of our faith. When they were getting ready to undertake a God project, fearfulness set in. Remember the earlier stories of Moses and Gideon.

Finally, our lack of peace can come from a lack of faith. Have we given God control of our lives, or are we constantly worried about what will happen next? Worry, anxiety, and panic are sometimes the result of refusing to hand over our problems to God, and trust that he can handle them all. Have you, as the Carrie Underwood song says, asked Jesus to take the wheel? If you have, do you keep grabbing the wheel back because of a lack of faith?

I recently started watching University of Iowa wrestling matches with my husband. It reminds me of the relationship we must have with fear. The primary goal for any wrestler is to pin his opponent to the mat. Then, the match is over. I can't believe the way wrestlers contort their bodies in order to win points. In our effort to achieve peace, we must wrestle with our unhealthy fears and anxieties so we can pin them to the mat. Match over!

If this opponent of ours is so much a part of our lives, why should we even bother with this struggle?

Scarf of Truth:
Fear feeds our insecurity.

We should wrestle with fear because this uneasiness and insecurity are like two pieces of twine woven together. They feed each other. They squash our peace. Where there is insecurity, there will always be anxiety lurking in the shadows. Think of your worries and how they influence your insecurity. Do you have a fear of spousal infidelity? Does it cause you to feel insecure in your marriage? Do you fret about how your kids will turn out? Does that make you feel insecure around other mothers with brilliant kids? Do you break out in a cold sweat at the thought of public speaking?

Danielle is a manager at her company, but because fear has such a grip on her, she has trouble sharing her ideas in meetings. This causes her to feel insecure about her job, her intelligence, and what others think of her. However, Danielle won't let this problem conquer her. She pushes herself to share ideas even when anxiety aims to win.

Scarf of Truth:
Many times, God reveals his plan for our lives in the unknown.

We must also wrestle with fear because it often drops in on us when we are in the land of the unknown. If we don't pin it down, we prevent God from blessing us in a unique situation.

Let's look at Peter's story in Matthew 14:22–33:

Immediately Jesus made the disciples get into the boat and go on ahead of him to the other side, while he dismissed the crowd. After he had dismissed them, he went up on a mountainside by himself to pray. Later that night, he was there alone, and the boat was already a considerable distance from land, buffeted by the waves because the wind was against it.

Shortly before dawn Jesus went out to them, walking on the lake. When the disciples saw him walking on the lake, they were terrified. "It's a ghost," they said, and cried out in fear.

But Jesus immediately said to them: "Take courage! It is I. Don't be afraid."

"Lord, if it's you," Peter replied, "Tell me to come to you on the water."

"Come," he said.

Then Peter got down out of the boat, walked on the water and came toward Jesus. But when he saw the wind, he was afraid and, beginning to sink, cried out, "Lord, save me!"

Immediately Jesus reached out his hand and caught him. "You of little faith," he said, "Why did you doubt?"

And when they climbed into the boat, the wind died down. Then those who were in the boat worshiped him, saying, "Truly you are the Son of God."

This great story not only focuses on Peter's fear, but it also speaks to the inaction of the other apostles in the boat. Take a seat in the boat with the disciples for just a minute and ride their waves of panic. Are they wondering what they got themselves into? At this point, they have an inclination of who Jesus is, but they don't know the whole story or the happy ending. It's a classic case of venturing into the unknown. The disciples have never witnessed anyone walking on the water before, so is their fear of the unknown super-gluing them to their seats?

Do you remember the movie, *Indiana Jones and the Last Crusade*? Indiana had instructions from a friar's journal that in order to cross the great lion head chasm and receive the prize, he had to take a leap of faith. Indiana hesitated to step off of what looked like a cliff. Sweating, shaking, he bravely lifted his foot and stepped out into the unknown. Suddenly, a previously invisible bridge of rock appeared before him—and he crossed over to safety.

I believe God will lead us to the edge of the unknown many times throughout our lives because that is where we are closest to him. We lean on him harder when we are in a situation where the ground is a little shaky below us, don't we? Looking back on my life, I realize that if I had not ventured into the unknown, I would have missed out on the direction God wanted me to take. If I had refused to move to Flower Mound, Texas, from San Antonio, a comfortable old shoe to live in, I would never have led women's ministry at our church or written this book. If Abraham had not obeyed God and left his cushy digs in Ur, the whole course of Bible history would have been different. Do you see that while the unknown is scary, it can hold many blessings for us if we choose to move forward?

Scarf of Truth:
Anything can become an idol when it takes God's place—even fear.

The final reason we must wrestle with fear is that we don't want it to take God's place. Exodus 20:4–5 calls anything that takes the place of God in our hearts an idol: "You shall not make for yourself an image in the form of anything in heaven above or on the earth beneath or in the waters below. You shall not bow down to them or worship them; . . ."

Obviously, it's not that we love our worries and anxieties more than God, but sometimes, we think about them too much, giving them more power. Fear has our attention, not God.

Fear had such a stranglehold on Tamara that she sought help by going to a church support group for anxiety and panic attacks. Sitting in a circle of chairs, Tamara listened to Rodney talk about his struggle with panic.

"I can't stand the feeling," Rodney said. "I'd do anything to avoid it."

As Tamara scanned the group of men and women, she knew everyone felt the same way. That was the problem.

"We would have done anything to avoid that panic feeling," Tamara said. "Avoiding the problem was more important than anything else."

Months later in a Bible study, another insight came when someone said, "You worship anything that controls your life." She realized that while the Israelites had built a calf and then offered sacrifices to it, she had made fear her idol and was bowing down to it daily.

"I offered up trips out with friends; getting to know new people; speaking in front of others; my potential career. I offered them all up to my idol of anxiety," Tamara explained.

Satan wants us to live a life thinking something is more powerful than God. God wants our time and talents, but fear can rip them out of his arms. The enemy wants us shivering in our boots in our homes, without peace, and unable to go out because of our anxieties. Fear in itself isn't wrong, but giving it too much power is. As the author Ambrose Redmoon once said, "Courage is not the absence of fear, but rather the judgment that something else is more important than fear." Yes, God is more important than fear. It seems obvious when we say it this way, but let's remember this in our day-to-day lives as we wrestle with our trembling hearts.

When we pin these paralyzing fears to the mat, we rise from the ranks of the defeated and raise our hands in victory.

Scarf of Truth:
On the path to peace, God will guide us every step of the way, one step at a time.

God often does not give us the entire road map. Instead, he doles out one small leg of our life journey at a time. We, on the other hand, like to know where we are going. Some of us have had our lives all planned out from the day we left home. But because we don't always know the final destination, we have to trust our holy driver, who has a better sense of direction than we do.

I'll always remember a story I read in *The Hiding Place* about a conversation the young Corrie Ten Boom had with her father. Corrie, who later survived the Nazi prison camps, told her father she feared death:

Father sat down on the edge of the narrow bed. "Corrie," he began gently, "when you and I go to Amsterdam—when do I give you the ticket?"

Corrie sniffed a few times, considering this, and answered. "Why, just before we get on the train."

"Exactly. And our wise Father in heaven knows when we're going to need things, too. Don't run out ahead of Him, Corrie. When the time comes that some of us will have to die, you will look into your heart and find the strength you need—just in time."[1]

Diane remembered how God, in his perfect timing, led her step-by-step to her next task. Years ago, she belonged to a group that made Christian jewelry to raise funds for missions. Then one day, she happened on a meeting about a mission trip to Mozambique. "I went in because they had spent so much time preparing the presentation, and hardly anyone showed." As it turned out, Diane was moved by the program and felt a tug to go to Africa, but wondered what she had to offer. The trip participants were all working on electrical and hospital undertakings, so she put her thought about Africa on the back burner.

A few years passed, and by then both of her kids were in college. The organizers of the African mission approached her. "The women in Mozambique are looking for something else to do to help their families. Could you teach the women how to make jewelry?" Now, that was something she could do!

She traveled to Mozambique that year to instruct the women in the trade, then started selling their jewelry back home, which led her to find new markets for the jewelry. Searching for new markets led Diane to open Mission Matters, a fair trade store and mission center at her church. That is where you'll find her today. But God did not give her a vision for the store early on; he gave her the pieces of her personal road map one leg at a time.

Scarf of Truth:
On the path to peace, our fear lessens to the degree we know God, choose to trust him, and believe he can heal us.

When you increase your faith, you will decrease your fear. When worry creeps into their bodies, children reach for security blankets, suck their thumbs, or grab the loving hand of a parent. As adults, we can learn to reach up and grab God's hand.

David, in Psalm 56:3, makes a decision to put his trust in the Lord: "When I am afraid, I put my trust in you."

Over the course of his life, Peter moved from fear to faith. This man who sank into the water when he saw waves, who denied Jesus three times before the cock crowed, ultimately died for his testimony. By the end of their lives, all the apostles were fearless. Why is that? Because after seeing God work in their lives, they knew he had their back, their front, and everything in between. They witnessed Jesus calming the seas, feeding the thousands, and healing the sick, and spent time with him after he was raised from the dead. Jesus had conquered it all; what else was there to worry about?

Like the disciples, Charlotte, a tap-dancing mother of two, had to move from fear to faith because when she was in her late forties, fear stole her livelihood away.

Charlotte recalls grocery shopping one day. Pushing the cart up and down the aisle, she suddenly felt a wave of intense fear. Nothing was wrong outside but inside she felt like a tiger trapped in a cage. She had to get out. Abandoning her groceries in the aisle, heart pounding, she raced home. For several years, her fear of repeating the anxiety was so great, she couldn't leave the house alone.

"I also had a fear of flying," she said. "My parents were flying a lot at the time and always offered to take me. I never went with them, and never told them why." Even though she was a Christian at this time, she didn't confide in anyone about her suffering—not even her husband. Why did she keep it a secret? "If you had fear and anxiety, people thought you didn't know how to trust the Lord. You, therefore, must not be Christian," she said. At the time, she could hardly concentrate enough to read the Bible, but she'd quote Scripture to herself and always had her praise music going. "I would put it in a cassette player and play it for hours."

During this time, Charlotte witnessed how God healed other people, and she believed with all her heart that God could heal her from fear, as well. "Believing that God can take you out of anything, including fear, is crucial," she said. God honored Charlotte's belief. "God slowly brought me out of it," she said. He removed her anxiety and many physical ailments over the years. Because of this, she now sees life from a more peaceful point of view. "Different things I have to do, like the shots I just had in my back, can make me fearful, but I don't fear those things anymore because I know that no matter what, God is there, and he's going to take care of me." Charlotte now helps others suffering from anxiety. "I sit and talk to them. I read to them. I write out Scriptures. I pray with people and tell them to listen to praise music, because these are the things that helped me."

God moved Charlotte from anxiety to peace.

We've all been in crisis situations and felt like the sinking Peter whom Jesus grabbed and pulled out of the water. After the crisis passed, we see how the hand of God brought us through the trial, and we think, "Wow, Lord, you really did get me through that one. I wish I wouldn't have reacted the way I did. If only I had trusted you!" Then, the next time something happens, we trust him a little bit more, fear loosens its hold on our lives, and peace can slip in between us and anxiety's icy grip.

Our peace will also increase when we realize the power of God's Word.

Scarf of Truth:
Having faith in God and in his Word can protect us from our fearful thoughts.

The Bible tells us time and time again to protect our minds because before we know it, our thoughts sneak in and steal our peace. In 1 Peter 5:8 God says, "Be alert and of sober mind. Your enemy the devil prowls around like a roaring lion looking for some-one to devour." Sometimes, though, we approach protecting our thoughts in the wrong way and try to stop them ourselves.

We all know it's impossible not to think of a pink elephant, but we still attempt the same approach when trying not to be anxiety ridden. A better strategy is to guard our thoughts. The act of guard-ing is putting something between our minds and the fearful thoughts. The Queen's Guard in London protects the royal family. These soldiers strut back-and-forth, placing themselves between the Queen and the commoners. So how do we put something between our mind and the thoughts that pierce us with projectile arrows of fear? We should make a shield and fashion it with God's Word, remind yourself of God's truth in your life, and pray. Ephesians 6:16 says, "In addition to all this, take up the shield of faith, with which you can extinguish all the flaming arrows of the evil one."

When you feel your heart and soul tremble, have Bible verses memorized or handy. They will shield you from fear so peace can prevail. For example:

Genesis 15:1: "Do not be afraid, Abram. I am your shield . . ."

Psalm 27:1: "The Lord is my light and my salvation—whom shall I fear?"

Psalm 56:11: "In God I trust and am not afraid. What can man do to me?"

Proverbs 4:23: "Above all else, guard your heart, for everything you do flows from it."

Philippians 4:13: "I can do all this through him who gives me strength."

2 Timothy 1:7: "For the Spirit God gave us does not make us timid, but gives us power, love and self-discipline."

Philippians 4:6: "Do not be anxious about anything, but in every situation, by prayer and petition, with thanksgiving, present your requests to God."

Ann remembered the Sunday afternoon when she used her shield of faith. Her family had headed out on a boat to do some tubing. "The weather seemed fine; we left the house, but by the time we got the boat launched and headed out to deep water, the skies were cloudy, and the wind was getting strong," Ann said.

The farther from shore they got, the windier it became, and soon, whitecaps tossed the boat from one side to the other. Frightened by the worsening situation, Ann prayed. "I couldn't quote chapter and verse, but I reminded God of how he parted the Red Sea, calmed the storm for Jesus to walk on water, and every other water-related Bible story I could remember," Ann said. She believed God could do the same for her, so she released her fear of the storm and put her faith in God to protect her. "Slowly, the wind began to calm, and the sun reappeared. It became as calm and as beautiful a day as you could imagine," Ann said. Everyone had a great time that day, and Ann renewed her faith in the Lord by turning her worry over to him and using her shield of faith.

Second, remind yourself of your faith journey and all the times God has come through for you. Let's call them "faith markers." In the Old Testament, when the patriarchs had a close encounter with God, they would build an altar at the site of the holy event to acknowledge what happened.

When you experience a brush with God's greatness, you should build an altar in your mind so you can return to our faith marker when your conviction wavers. If it's difficult to remember all the times God has come through for you, start writing them down. Also, listen to or read other people's faith stories. Don't look at the unstable waters looming below. Think about all the times God has rescued you. Faith trumps fear.

Finally, pray and praise God even in the hard times as it says in Psalm 34:4: "I sought the LORD, and he answered me; he delivered me from all my fears."

Scarf of Truth:
Perfect love casts out fear.

In 1 John 4:18, the *New King James Version,* it says, "There is no fear in love; but perfect love casts out fear: because fear involves torment. But he who fears has not been made perfect in love."

Does this verse mean we are supposed to have no fear if we know God and love him? I don't believe it does. "Cast" means to throw or hurl: to fling. It means to get rid of something. It says nothing about it not being there in the first place. Fearful thoughts will come into our mind, but if we focus on love, they will be cast out before they become unmanageable.

Rhonda remembered how perfect love cast out her fear.

Pacing in the L.A. airport, preparing for their flight to China to adopt their first child, Rhonda voiced her concern to her husband. "I'm not sure I can do this," she said speaking of their looming fourteen-hour plane ride. Rhonda had suffered from anxiety and panic attacks for three years. How could she, a person who suffered from claustrophobia, be on an airplane for fourteen hours?

The ride west across the ocean was an exhausting struggle of keeping the panic at bay. On the way home, with their newly adopted baby in her arms, she didn't even think about being anxious. She was so busy loving and caring for the baby, the time flew by. Rhonda's love for her new baby cast out all her fear.

Research backs up experience in this matter. A number of studies, including one at Massachusetts Institute of Technology, found that, for the most part, people can't focus on more than one thing at a time. If we concentrate on love and appreciation, our fear cannot remain.

Few will ever forget the tragic events of September 11, 2001. Do you remember where you were on that day? I was the spokesperson for an airport, and soon after the planes crashed, we were holding a press conference with the media and the Director of the

Airport, Chief of Airport Police, and others on hand to answer the media's questions.

There was a lot of uncertainty on that day and the days to follow, wasn't there? The crazy thing is I had to speak on the subject of "balance" two days later at a sold-out Christian event. I didn't think I could do it. After 9/11, I was the most unbalanced I'd ever been in my life. The press called me non-stop. I was interviewed live on morning shows, noon shows, and evening newscasts. As late as the day of the event, I was talking myself out of doing the presentation because I just couldn't focus. That morning, a policeman stopped by where I was standing on the sidewalk at the airport and asked whether I needed a police escort down to my speaking event, which was close to downtown, twenty minutes from the airport. I thought, *If God can provide a police escort, I can do the talk.*

I don't even remember what I said that day. I only know that I took my eyes off my fears and circumstances and moved them to what God wanted me to do, which I believe was to present his message, and he accomplished the task through me. It was truly an out-of-body experience. I remember the event organizer counted me down to let me know I was out of time. Five, four, three, two, one, and I was finished. Perfectly on time. That day, perfect love cast out my fear.

With everything going on in the world around you, no one can blame you for entertaining fears, but if debilitating fear has a hold of your life, God has given you the ability to pin it to the mat. Match over!

Gloves of Prayer: *Gracious God, you are a God of peace, not fear. I want to trust you with my life more and fear less. Please take fear off the throne of my life and replace it with your peace. When I become anxious, remind me to immediately pray and give my anxiety over to you. Help me know beyond a shadow of a doubt that when you are with me, there is no reason to fear. In Jesus' name, AMEN.*

Discussion Questions:
If I Only Had . . . Peace

1. Most of us had fears as a young child. What were your fears as you grew up? What fears have you grown out of and what caused you to see those previous fears in a more realistic light?

2. Some fears are natural, immediate, and an intense reaction to danger. Other fears come from our past experiences or are fears of the future. What fears rob you of peace as an adult? Can you allow God to give you a different perspective on those fears?

3. Satan delights when we are too scared to act. Describe a time when fear caused you to be too afraid to act.

4. Fear and insecurity are like two pieces of twine woven together. How does fear feed your insecurity?

5. A wrestler's primary goal is to pin his opponent to the mat. In a wrestling match between you and fear, how would you react? Bow down to it? Talk back to it? Run from it? Let it do anything it wants to your life? Pin it to the mat? Do you listen to fear only when it is in line with God's word?

6. We must wrestle with fear for three reasons: to prevent fear from becoming an idol, because God reveals his plan for our lives in the unknown, and because fear will otherwise feed our insecurity. Which of these reasons speaks to you? Describe a fear you wrestled with, and explain why you decided to ignore the voice of fear.

7. Jesus invited Peter to step out of the boat and walk with him on water. When have you seen God guiding you one step at a time instead of giving you the long-term plan?

8. Charlotte, a tap-dancing mother of two, suffered from panic attacks for years until God moved her from anxiety to peace. Has God healed you of any fears? What fears do you still need to place firmly in his hands?

9. As it says in 1 John 4:18, "Perfect love casts out fear." When fearful thoughts come, and they will come, what practical steps can you take to cast them out with love?

10. In an effort to trump fear with faith, think of a few times God has rescued you. Mark these experiences by building an altar in your mind so you can remember what God has done for you.

Four

If I Only Had ...
Dignity

I EMBRACE EVERYTHING ABOUT being a woman except for our hormones. This year, I entered the mother lode of all hormonal issues, the pause. After my doctor gave me the news, I sailed through for a while; for seven months, I enjoyed the freedom of skipping my time of the month. Figuring it was awkward to donate my monthly supplies to a friend, I was about to throw them away when it hit again with a fury. And it kept on hitting, and hitting and hitting. Every day, I asked, "When is this going to end?"

I finally called my OB/GYN, and the unworried nurse said, "It's all a part of being a woman. You may stop in a day or so, then start right back up next week."

Wrong answer! I don't want to live my life thinking the tidal wave could come at any minute.

Is this how the hemorrhaging woman in the Bible lived?

Later that day, I received a call from the doctor's office. This time, the same nurse seemed more concerned. She told me the doctor wanted me to come in for some blood work and a sonogram, just to make sure.

The day of the appointment, after the sonogram, the doctor

came in to deliver the results with a long, worried face. I knew it was not great news. She told me the lining of my uterus was four times thicker than they liked to see. A biopsy needed to be done right away.

"Right now?" I didn't even have time to worry and sweat it out. Apparently, a thick uterine lining is one of the indications of endometrial cancer.

"Oh, and by the way, this will cause more bleeding."

Oh, no, I thought. *I am going to have to go back to the store and get more supplies.*

Worries, inconvenience, and weakness—the woman who bled for twelve years had all these issues and more. When I think of the absence of dignity, I always recall this particular woman in the Bible. As I began to write this chapter, God, in his perfect timing, gave me a small window into her world.

Imagine what it must have been like for this woman to suffer with hormonal issues day after day, wondering whether the flow would ever stop. She was concerned about her health and probably spent a lot of money on doctors or faith healers, none of whom helped her.

We find her story in Luke 8:42–47:

As Jesus was on his way, the crowds almost crushed him. And a woman was there who had been subject to bleeding for twelve years, but no one could heal her. She came up behind him and touched the edge of his cloak, and immediately her bleeding stopped.

"Who touched me?" Jesus asked.

When they all denied it, Peter said, "Master, the people are crowding and pressing against you."

But Jesus said, "Someone touched me; I know that power has gone out from me."

Then the woman, seeing that she could not go unnoticed, came trembling and fell at his feet.

This woman had lost her dignity, and Jesus was her last hope for healing.

Scarf of Truth:
When we lose our dignity, we should reach out to Jesus first, not last.

Have you ever been sick and didn't want anyone to know? Did you go to doctor after doctor trying to find a remedy, but no one could help you? Then, at the eleventh hour, you decided to seek friends to pray for you? After the prayer chain got started, suddenly you experienced some health changes and a turnaround in your situation. What made the difference? You reached out to touch Jesus.

I know someone whose husband was diagnosed with brain cancer. Because he was only in his fifties, the diagnosis shocked everyone around him. He had nine months to live, maybe a year. Unfortunately, in his mind, this man lost his dignity because of the illness. After rounds of treatment, he gave up church, worried that people stared at his hairless head.

During the course of his illness, I learned about a study being conducted in California that examined the impact of prayer on cancer patients. In this study, a group prayed daily for one-half of the cancer patients. The other cancer patients were not prayed for. During the process, none of the cancer patients knew to which group they belonged. I asked my friend whether she wanted her husband to be part of the group. Unfortunately, she wanted nothing to do with the study. She simply chose to accept the prognosis and make her husband as comfortable as possible in his last months.

If you were the woman bleeding for twelve years, would you give up and accept your condition? Who could blame you if you did? Yet, instead of throwing in the towel, this woman, weak from her condition, battled crushing crowds to touch the edge of Jesus' cloak. This woman had heard and believed that Jesus could change her life. She knew that what others saw as impossible was right up Jesus' alley.

Scarf of Truth:
Jesus has the ability to heal us from our illnesses.

Jesus doesn't cure every illness, but he did heal the hemorrhaging woman and still heals people today. I have witnessed both physical and emotional healing through prayer. In our Sunday school class, a man with a staph infection was at the point of having his leg amputated. In an effort to help him with home improvements, one day, our class painted the interior of his house. While there, we prayed over his leg. We prayed, believing Jesus could heal him even though doctors had essentially given up hope of saving his leg.

What happened afterward was a miracle! Our classmate made a rapid recovery, and then the staph infection disappeared. Just like the woman who bled for twelve years, this man finally reached out to touch Jesus, and Jesus' healing power touched him back.

I don't think the woman who touched Jesus' cloak lost her dignity just because of the bleeding. First, because of her non-stop flow, she was probably infertile. A twelve-year stretch without pregnancy would have been crushing in ancient Galilee. Back then, being fruitful and multiplying, as God commanded, was a woman's job. This woman was cut off from motherhood, the task that gave her life meaning and provided her acceptable social status in her community.

The second devastating consequence for this woman was she was perpetually unclean. We certainly don't think that way today, do we?

Sorry, I can't attend the party; it's one of my unclean days.

Thankfully, we are no longer excluded from Sunday worship

and other religious events when we're in our ritually polluted time of the month.

In her day, this uncleanness also passed on like a bad cold. Anyone who touched this woman would be deemed unclean, as if infected. Her husband, if she had one, certainly could not have been intimate with her for twelve years. This woman was probably a lonely outcast. She couldn't go to temple, and my guess is no one came knocking on her door.

The same friend of mine whose husband had cancer shared that many of her friends never came to visit them during her husband's sickness. As the woman with the issue of blood experienced, isolation and loneliness sometimes accompany illness and pain.

Scarf of Truth:
When we feel alone and isolated, Jesus can give us hope.

When everyone else abandoned her, the hemorrhaging woman saw hope in Christ, but seeking after him wasn't without risk. Imagine the scene: Unclean, she touches everyone as she squeezes through the middle of the crowd. Perspiration drips down her forehead as she considers what will happen if someone notices her where she is not supposed to be. She discovers Jesus, just ahead. With a fierce desire to regain her dignity, she reaches for his cloak and grasps the corner. His healing floods her body; the blood dries up. Overjoyed, she attempts to melt back into the crowd, and then, she hears the words, "Who touched me?"

Oh, no! This is not what she wanted to happen. She knows that, according to Jewish law, she has done something wrong by reaching out and touching a holy person. Still bent over, she struggles with what to do. She isn't privy to what you know about Jesus. She doesn't know he healed a leper, also considered unclean. There was no newspaper headline informing her he cleansed a woman tormented by seven demons. She doesn't realize Jesus is willing and ready to reach out and touch her.

Scarf of Truth:
Jesus wants to reach out and touch everyone.

It doesn't matter what you are going through or how awful and unclean you feel; Jesus wants to heal you. Remember the Pharisees quizzing Jesus about his choice of company in Matthew 9:10–13:

> While Jesus was having dinner at Matthew's house, many tax collectors and sinners came and ate with him and his disciples. When the Pharisees saw this, they asked his disciples, "Why does your teacher eat with tax collectors and sinners?"
>
> On hearing this, Jesus said, "It is not the healthy who need a doctor, but the sick. But go and learn what this means: 'I desire mercy, not sacrifice.' For I have not come to call the righteous, but sinners."

Jesus didn't hang out with the cream of the crop. He says directly he came to help those that needed help. He healed a demon-possessed woman. He saved the life of an adulterous woman. He cured the sick, gave vision to the blind, and he can heal you as well, both physically and emotionally, from your current wounds and the wounds of the past.

Leah needed healing from her past wounds of physical and psychological abuse.

Leah recalled the night something changed inside of her. She came home past her curfew because a car accident had blocked traffic. Everyone knew how her mom was, so her friends came into her house to explain it wasn't Leah's fault they were late. "When we walked in, my mom got up from her chair, and, without waiting to hear why I was past curfew, she slapped me as hard as she could across the face in front of my friends," Leah said.

"I started to cry, and then I felt something within me die," she said. She had always wanted her mother's love but instead received destructive words such as, "Go, away," and, "Why would anyone ever want to be your friend?" Her mother refused to give her dignity.

"That night something in me said, *I'll never let anyone hurt me like that again.*"

However, Jesus resurrected what died in Leah. He touched Leah's life and gave back her dignity by providing her the ability to love again. He blessed her with three beautiful children and dignity through motherhood. Through his restoration of her life, she is the mom she never had. "I broke the cycle."

Leah is there for her children, and while she says she is not perfect, "My kids have always known that they are loved." Leah learned that often, God uses the bad in our lives for good and in this way begins to restore our dignity.

Scarf of Truth:
If God is to restore our dignity and provide healing, we must be transparent before him.

When the hemorrhaging woman knew she could not slip away, she fell at Jesus' feet; trembling, she told him everything. She laid her soul bare, explaining why she had touched him, and confirmed her healing.

You want to be transparent, with no hidden agendas between you and Christ. He knows everything, so be honest in your prayers for healing. Maybe there is some nasty habit you cannot kick. You may hide it from everyone else, but God knows all about it. There is a famous line in Alcoholics Anonymous that each new member needs to say, "Hello, my name is Jane Smith, and I am an alcoholic."

When we try to cover up our issues, the light of God's healing cannot reach them. Once we are honest with ourselves and him, then he can get down to work. It's time for healing.

Scarf of Truth:
We are all daughters of God.

When the woman admitted to Jesus she had touched him, he didn't yell at her and say, *What were you doing, foolish woman! Don't you know I'm a rabbi as well as the Son of God? How dare you touch me?* When we've lost our dignity, that's what we often expect, but with Jesus, it wasn't like that at all. I imagine him looking into her eyes with a hint of a smile, saying, "Daughter, your faith has healed you. Go in peace." (Luke 8:48)

Tears came to her eye at his tenderness. No one had treated her so kindly in twelve years, and here was this man with the amazing power of God calling her "daughter."

John 1:12,13 confidently states, "Yet to all who did receive him, to those who believed in his name, he gave the right to become children of God—children born not of natural descent, nor of human decision or a husband's will, but born of God."

If we are children of God, that makes us daughters of God. Do you claim God as your Father? Do you know how much God loves you? Do you realize how much Jesus loves you? Jesus had never met the woman who touched his cloak in the crowd, but he knew what she had been through. He loved her enough to consider her a daughter, the same way he considers you and me his daughters. What an honor and a privilege to be an adopted daughter of God. After Jesus and the woman, now whole, wrapped up their encounter, Jesus leaves her with these words: "Your faith has healed you, go in peace."

Scarf of Truth:
It takes faith to regain our dignity and receive healing.

As I told you at the beginning of this chapter, God gave me a personal experience that enabled me to understand just a snippet of what this woman was feeling. After my biopsy, I had about five days to think about the "what ifs."

"What if I do have cancer and need surgery right away?" It deeply distressed me that I might miss a couple weeks of a Bible study I was leading.

I'm sure at that point, God was saying, *Oh, you of little faith! Didn't I call you to teach that study?* The following weekend, I was supposed to attend my cousin's wedding in California. *Would I be all down in the mouth and not have a good time if it was bad news? What if it was the worst case scenario? How much time would I have to get my affairs in order?* I immediately thought of my messy closet.

While my faith was weak in some areas, in this instance it was strong. The one thing I knew, as did the woman in Luke's account, was that Jesus could heal me if I was sick; I just needed to reach out and touch his cloak, figuratively speaking.

The way I touched Jesus' cloak was to text the prayer warriors in my life, asking them to pray for healing. I also asked my Sunday school class to pray for the biopsy to be negative.

When Wednesday came around, I did get the call from the doctor's office, and the nurse I'd spoken with earlier turned out to be right; it was just part of being a woman. Was I healed by Jesus? I don't know the answer to that. What I do know beyond a shadow of doubt is that Jesus healed the woman who bled for twelve long years, and Jesus is still able to heal you and me.

What do you need healing from? Is it a physical ailment? Emotional trauma? Insecurity? Do you have a damaged soul? Whatever your wounds, you can learn from the hemorrhaging woman.

Imagine a package sitting on a shelf. The gift tag reads To: You,

From: Jesus. For some people, it sits on the shelf unopened, collecting dust; for others, it's battered; others have taken it down and given it away; still others don't see the parcel. They don't believe they are worthy of the gift. Everyone has received this gift, but only a few open it and keep it as the cherished gift it is. Inside the package is your dignity, your worthiness, your God-given nobility. What have you done with your gift? Have you let someone or something take it away?

Reach out to touch Jesus, and don't let the crowd stop you.

Pursue him through Bible studies, prayers, and worship.

Believe he can and wants to help you.

Put your hope in him.

Be transparent before him.

Finally, reach up, see the gift labeled To: you, From: Jesus.

Grab it off the shelf, and claim your place in his holy family.

Gloves of Prayer: *Father, when I am sick and need healing, help me to reach out and touch your cloak first, not last. Like the woman who bled for twelve straight years, I want to humble myself and seek Jesus' touch by asking the body of Christ to pray for me. No matter what has attempted to destroy my dignity, help me to remember I am your daughter and my hope is in you. In Jesus' name, AMEN.*

Discussion Questions:
If I Only Had . . . Dignity

1. As women we can identify with the hemorrhaging woman and how undignified she must have felt. Have you ever experienced a loss of dignity, or felt that a person or a situation was undermining your sense of dignity? If so, how did it impact you?

2. When we lose our dignity, we should reach out to Jesus first. Have you ever gone from doctor to doctor trying to find a remedy for your illness, but no one could help? Then, at the eleventh hour, you decided to seek friends to pray for you? When going through a difficult trial, to whom do you go first for help? If Jesus is not your first choice, why not?

3. Luke 8:42–47 tells the story of how Jesus healed the woman who bled for twelve years straight. In the final scene "she came up behind Jesus and touched the edge of his cloak, and immediately her bleeding stopped." How do you know that Jesus still heals?

4. When everyone else abandoned her, the hemorrhaging woman saw hope in Christ. Have you ever been in a place where all your prospects seemed gone? What and who restored your hope? How does Jesus give you hope?

5. Leah needed healing from her past wounds of physical and psychological abuse. What physical, psychological, spiritual, or emotional wounds could you bring to God for healing?

6. Sometimes God's emotional and spiritual healing is instant while at other times it's gradual as he heals each layer of

pain. When healing takes time, we need to rely on God to get us through. How has God comforted you in affliction?

7. Jesus wants to reach out and touch you. Do you believe that Jesus would take the time to stop in the middle of preaching, while surrounded by a crowd of people, and heal you? Take a moment and prayerfully imagine him doing this. How did this make you feel?

8. When the hemorrhaging woman knew she could not slip away, she fell at Jesus' feet; trembling, she told him everything. Are you honest in your prayers about your need for healing? Do you come to God as you are, or do you try to be the person you think he wants you to be before approaching him?

9. Jesus called the hemorrhaging woman "daughter." In John 1:12,13 God's Word confirms we are all children of God: "Yet to all who did receive him, to those who believed in his name, he gave the right to become children of God— children born not of natural descent, nor of human decision or a husband's will, but born of God." Do you claim this promise from God? How does it make you feel to know you are a daughter of God?

10. The hemorrhaging woman knew all she needed for healing was to touch Jesus' cloak. What action do you need to take to be whole again?

Five

If I Only Had . . .
A Brain

JOAN REMEMBERED ONE AWFUL day in grade school when her teacher called her to the blackboard to write the "four times tables." A hearing problem brought on by a childhood illness had made Joan a poor student.

She stood there for what seemed like hours, nose to the black board, white chalk in hand.

"I didn't remember the times tables. No, to be honest, I did not know them," Joan said.

After several minutes, the teacher strolled to the board. She grabbed the chalk and wrote, "4 x 1 = 4. 4 x 2 = 8. 4 x 3 = 12." As one hand wrote on the blackboard, her other fist pounded Joan's back "4 x 4=16, 4 x 5=20 . . ."

Tears of humiliation and pain made tracks down Joan's cheeks.

Out of the corner of her eyes she saw girls with perfectly combed pigtails and perfectly tied pink ribbons, giggling as they sat perfectly upright in their desks. After her teacher finished writing "4 x 12= 48", she gave Joan one more whack.

Turning from the blackboard, the teacher smiled at her perfectly behaved students.

"Go to the bathroom and wash your dirty face," her teacher leered.

Moments like this gave Joan the "dumb kid" label from grade school all the way through high school. But God worked in her life to remove the label. "It wasn't until I joined the Navy at eighteen years old that I found out how smart I truly am," Joan said. While working as a data processor in the Navy, she went to college at the same time. After graduation, she excelled at this work and moved up the ranks from computer programmer to supervisory computer specialist.

"To this day," Joan said, "when Satan's trying to bug me, he throws the 'dumb kid' tag in my face. With God's help, I'm able to recognize this as Satan's ploy," Joan said. God reminds her how far he's brought her and what he wants her to do with her prior experiences. After Joan retired, God called her to become a writer and share her past struggles. She thinks it's funny God directed her to the very thing that used to be her worst subject. With her new call to be a writer, God gave her the ability and wisdom to see herself as he sees her. Joan is now one of the "smart kids" both in her own eyes and God's. To her God is the Great Recycler, because he never throws anything away and is always using our previous experiences for good, if we let him.

When it comes to intelligence, where do you imagine you fall? Do you feel more like Einstein or the scarecrow from *The Wizard of Oz* who believed he'd be complete if he only had a brain?

Most of us, like Joan, can recall times we haven't felt so smart.

I remember when I was a 22-year-old intern at a television station. I wrote a sports story and innocently gave it a title that had a different connotation. The news producer pasted a copy of the story on the wall as an example of what not to do. While my name was taken off the top of the page, everyone could deduce it was my report. I was embarrassed because my naive mistake was labeled as "dumb." It would have been better if the producer had spoken to me individually rather than make me a public spectacle.

However, I learned from the experience and continued on to have a broadcasting career.

Scarf of Truth:
We are intelligent in different ways, according to our God-given talents.

If you think of two intelligent people, chances are they won't be gifted the same way. God made us unique, from our fingertips, to our IQ, to our skills. While we normally think of intelligence as book smarts and memory, it is far more. A person's brainpower can range from remembering names to solving math problems, from artistic creativity to composing songs. The list is endless.

When the Israelites constructed the temple, a God of detail provided an intricate list of tasks a mile long, but he also supplied workers with the needed knowledge to get the job done.

As it says in Exodus 31:1–6:

> Then the LORD said to Moses, "See, I have chosen Bezalel son of Uri, the son of Hur, of the tribe of Judah, and I have filled him with the Spirit of God, with wisdom, with understanding, with knowledge, and with all kinds of skills—to make artistic designs for work in gold, silver and bronze, to cut and set stones, to work in wood, and to engage in all kinds of crafts. Moreover, I have appointed Oholiab son of Ahisamak, of the tribe of Dan, to help him. Also I have given ability to all the skilled workers to make everything I have commanded you: . . ."

Exodus goes on to describe the skills God gave to the other workers. God gave the Israelites wisdom, knowledge, and skills to do everything he needed them to do.

Erin, a 43-year-old woman, remembered the math class she nearly failed in high school. No matter how hard she tried, none of the formulas or algebraic expressions sank in. Still below the passing grade at the end of the semester, Erin asked her teacher for extra credit. Even today, the memory of her teacher's hurtful reply still stings: "I'll pass you if you promise never to take a class with me again." Her teacher's discouraging words never left her. Over twenty years later, Erin still believes she has no mind for math.

Sue, a grandmother of five, reminisced about her high school Latin class with Father Turza, who loved perfection as much as his Czechoslovakian garlic pancakes. She remembered him handing back her first test with red marks covering the page. The grade in the top right hand corner was a zero. She now wonders how anyone could get that low a grade. That day, a tearful Sue convinced both herself and her parents she couldn't pass Latin. She dropped the class.

Over the years, these two women discovered they were intelligent in other areas. Erin found out she possessed the formula for making people laugh, not for math. Sue figured out her emotional IQ soared higher than her Latin ability. They realized they were smart in different ways and created to accomplish the tasks God had called them to perform.

Scarf of Truth:
Wisdom is not the same as intelligence.

We all know instinctively that this is true. You may have met people with a low IQ who always have a wise word, and people with doctorates who don't know how to get along with others. Wisdom can be as far from intelligence as the east is from the west. The Hebrew word for wisdom is *kok-maw*, which means to be wise in thought and deed.

Wisdom begins with knowing what is right according to God and ends with action. Intelligence has to do with our own capacity, while wisdom has to do with having God's perspective and using it to bless others.

Wisdom is mentioned over 200 times in the Bible. Clearly, it is an important quality to God. Wisdom is so important, in fact, that God gave us specific instruction on how to attain it, starting with where wisdom begins.

Scarf of Truth:
Wisdom is birthed through a healthy fear of the Lord.

Psalm 111:10 says, "The fear of the LORD is the beginning of wisdom; all who follow his precepts have good understanding."

The Bible advises us many times to fear the Lord. Deuteronomy 6:24 says: "The LORD commanded us to obey all these decrees and to fear the LORD our God, so that we might always prosper and be kept alive, as is the case today." Isaiah 33:6 says: "He will be the sure foundation for your times, a rich store of salvation and wisdom and knowledge; the fear of the LORD is the key to this treasure."

Years ago on a trip to Yellowstone, a friend's family became aware of the potential dangers of not having a healthy fear of wild animals. While out hiking one day, they passed a man coaxing his four-year-old child toward a wild elk as the majestic animal munched grass. The dad saw Santa's Dasher in his mind's eye and wanted a keepsake picture. My friend's husband commented as they passed, "That's a wild animal, you know, and people get impaled with antlers every year." The dad lacked a healthy fear of what wild meant when considering elk. Thankfully, his child survived.

Later that day, as a coyote crossed their path, their own four-year-old daughter took off running after the cute "doggie" so she could pet him. They caught up to her before the coyote caught her scent. She, too, lacked a healthy fear of wild animals. Prior to this trip, her exposure to animals had consisted of pets and animals in the zoo.

We don't fear wild animals when we imagine them to be the same as docile pets. We fear them when we know their true nature. A healthy fear of God starts with knowing him. I think we often forget how big and powerful our God is because we are too busy making him our friend and prayer answerer.

Examples in the Bible abound of people receiving discipline because of their disrespect for God. We'd do well to stand up and take notice. One of the most famous passages spotlights Ananias and Sapphira, two early followers of Christ, who sold all their possessions to give the money to the church. But Ananias tried to pull a fast one on God. When he sold his possessions, he kept back a portion of it and lied about it. Acts 5:4–5 shows Peter's response to Ananias, and the rest of the story. "'Didn't it belong to you before it was sold? And after it was sold, wasn't the money at your disposal? What made you think of doing such a thing? You have not lied just to human beings but to God.' When Ananias heard this, he fell down and died. And great fear seized all who heard what had happened."

Proverbs 8:13 says: "To fear the LORD is to hate evil; I hate pride and arrogance, evil behavior and perverse speech."

We fear the Lord by detesting sin and evil. We fear the Lord when we dread separation from him. We fear the Lord when we reverently respect the God who is *I Am*. We fear the Lord when we put our fear in the right place and watch our other fears become smaller.

Scarf of Truth:
God will give you wisdom if you seek it.

Benjamin Franklin said, "Early to bed and early to rise, makes a man healthy, wealthy and wise." It's a catchy saying, but in 1 Kings 3:5–15, Solomon had a better plan as he lay on a mat with the city of Gibeon all around him. Solomon tossed and turned that night as he thought about his new job as king of Israel. Solomon loved his father and missed him. His father, David, had been the king of all kings. He remembered the song sung of David's mastery on the battlefield. "Saul has slain thousands and David his ten thousands." (1 Samuel 21:11) David had been the king that Israel needed, a great military leader, and a man after God's own heart. Now, Solomon didn't feel up to the task.

In and out of a restless sleep, Solomon moaned. A light drove out all the tension. Solomon's tossing stopped. His breathing evened. God's voice spoke clearly. "Ask! What shall I give you?" God put no conditions on the request. What should he ask for? Others might have hesitated, but Solomon knew right away what he wanted. He wanted to be a great king.

"So give your servant a discerning heart to govern your people and to distinguish between right and wrong," he asks God in 1 Kings 3:9. "For who is able to govern this great people of yours?"

Pleased, God replies in 1 Kings 3:12: "I will do what you have asked. I will give you a wise and discerning heart, so that there will never have been anyone like you, nor will there ever be."

God, of course, did as he promised and 1 King 4:29–34 talks about the miraculous wisdom of Solomon: "God gave Solomon wisdom and very great insight, and a breadth of understanding as measureless as the sand on the seashore."

Solomon would have blown the competition away on a trivia game show. He was a revered author, penning 3,000 proverbs, and was at the top of the Billboard charts, writing over a thousand songs. He could speak authoritatively on any subject, whether it be animals, birds, reptiles, or fish. He was more famous than Tom Cruise or Brad Pitt, and people saddled up their camels and traveled long distances to hear what he had to say. "From all nations people came to listen to Solomon's wisdom, sent by all the kings of the world, who heard of his wisdom."

Solomon's wisdom was and still is famous, but what does that mean for us commoners? Is God's promise only for the royal? No. God's promise of wisdom is for all believers. Proverbs 2:1–5 encourages us to store up God's commands within us and to search for wisdom as for hidden treasure: "then you will understand the fear of the LORD and find the knowledge of God."

If we seek wisdom as if for silver and treasure and cry out for it, we will receive it. This speaks to how valuable wisdom is and the passion with which God wants us to pursue it. But how do we pursue it with passion?

In the end, Solomon, emptied his storehouse of God's commands and exchanged God's wisdom for sensual pleasures: "He had seven hundred wives of royal birth and three hundred concubines, and his wives led him astray." (1 Kings 11:3)

Distracted by pleasures of the flesh, he discarded his wisdom and lost God's protection over his kingdom. We also can be easily distracted by the pleasures of this world and forget about our pursuit of wisdom.

Scarf of Truth:
Our wisdom grows by continually filling ourselves with God's wisdom.

Staying steadily on wisdom's path and continuing to grow in it is an ongoing process. What an opportunity. God, the creator of the universe, wrote a book with a generous helping of his wisdom. Do we realize what a colossal gift this is? Clearly not, because many of us rarely open the Bible, or we grudgingly study it just to get the assignment done.

Contrast this to the hours we spend watching TV and surfing the Internet. In a recent survey by EMarketer, the average adult spends about four-and-a-half hours per day watching television and two-and-a-half hours online.[1] This is a whopping forty-eight hours per week—more than a full-time job. It is estimated that reading the whole Bible takes just ninety hours. Surely we can give up some of our TV time for God's instruction book for life. Even Jesus studied the Old Testament writings that would one day make up the Bible as we know it today.

My friend, Kim, remembered joining a study that had her read through the Bible in one year. At first, none of it made sense. "I hated the Old Testament. It seemed dull and boring, and I rarely got anything out of it," she said. "But the longer I was faithful, the more I gleaned from the reading. Now, I even enjoy the book of Numbers."

This is true of anything we do, including studying the Bible. When my son first started to play the saxophone, it was all squeaks and squawks. He begged to quit. I made him stick it out until the end of the year and then let him decide whether to continue taking lessons the following year. By then he could play some songs, saw the value of playing an instrument, and wanted to continue. We don't often see the value of practicing an instrument at first. The same is true of God's Word. Value comes with the commitment to continually fill ourselves with his Word.

Scarf of Truth:
Our wisdom increases when we wholeheartedly trust in the Lord rather than rely on our own understanding.

Proverbs 3:5–6 says: "Trust in the LORD with all your heart and lean not on your own understanding; in all your ways submit to him, and he will make your paths straight."

Trusting in the Lord means listening to God's instruction whether you understand it or not. Know-it-alls are annoying because, in their opinion, they have nothing to learn. Are you teachable? Do you let God teach you through his Word and your circumstances?

Not relying on your own understanding means when something bad happens, you trust God will see you through the scenario and believe his perspective is more encompassing than yours. Consider this carefully. We've all been there. A parent dies, and we feel so alone. Whom do we trust? Our feelings of aloneness, or God saying he is always with us? Do our thoughts urge us to leave our marriage because it seems dull and lifeless, or do we believe God's Word when he says marriage is a covenant? We feel life isn't worth living. Do we trust our feelings or believe God has a plan to give us a future and hope? There is a plethora of things we cannot or will never understand, but fortunately, our God does.

Nowhere is this more evident than in our experiences with being Spirit-led. Frankly, being led by the Spirit doesn't make a lot of rational sense, but if you've ever felt it, you know it's real.

Think of the apostles, sitting in the upper room with fear in their hearts, waiting for a gift from God. The wind picked up and fire swooped in, landing like tongues on the crowns of every head. Did they say, *I don't understand what is going on, and frankly, it's all too weird?* If so, they would have missed a huge opportunity.

The same is true for us. Every time the Spirit tries to lead us and we don't follow because we don't understand, we are the ones who miss out. The apostles were ordinary men used by God to birth the church of Jesus Christ—a church that would spread God's truth to the four corners of the globe. We, too, are ordinary people with extraordinary potential. With God's power and wisdom, we can do amazing acts.

Scarf of Truth:
God's wisdom working in our life
will make us more like Christ.

God's wisdom will purify us and help our faith grow. It will change us from the inside out, helping us to take on the qualities Christ himself possessed. Do you believe this? What is wisdom worth if it doesn't lead to personal transformation?

If we have accepted Jesus as our Savior, the Holy Spirit and his wisdom reside in us. Let's take a few moments to consider how his wisdom will change every aspect of who we are, starting at the top.

EYES AND EARS

How will God's wisdom change our eyes and ears? Isaiah 6:9 says: "Be ever hearing, but never understanding; be ever seeing, but never perceiving." This is how we are before God's wisdom enters our lives. We have a choice in every situation; sometimes we purposely blind ourselves to others' pain and suffering so we don't have to act. Children cover their ears and sing when they don't want to hear; adults turn on the TV, don't answer the phone, or keep the conversation light when talking with a friend who really needs a listening ear.

Wisdom will make both our eyes and ears sharper. I asked an extremely intelligent friend why an owl is considered wise. She immediately replied, "Because they don't speak, and they sit on a lofty branch simply observing what's going on."

People who are wise not only see what is going on, they perceive what is happening in the background. They notice the person on the sidelines with his head down, trying to be invisible but inwardly wanting to be included. They care about the lonely neighbor. They understand the child without friends. People with wisdom not only hear what is said, they understand the real meaning. They notice when a friend's "I'm fine" has a hint of sadness, so they stop to get the rest of the story. Proverbs 20:12 says: "Ears that hear and eyes that see—the LORD has made them both."

Wise people have learned by the Spirit to interpret people and situations from God's point of view.

THE MOUTH

How will God's wisdom change your speech? The Greek philosopher Zeno said, "The reason we have two ears and only one mouth, is that we may hear more and speak less."[2] Few of us take these words of wisdom to heart. Psalm 37:30 says: "The mouths of the righteous utter wisdom, and their tongues speak what is just."

Intellectually, we may know God's standard for good and

upright speech. But in reality, our mouths are often out of our control. Do you gossip about a neighbor? Do you cut down your spouse? Do you use angry words with relatives?

What should we do about controlling our speech? The Bible's advice is clear. Ephesians 4:29 says, "Do not let any unwholesome talk come out of your mouths, but only what is helpful for building others up according to their needs, that it may benefit those who listen." Proverbs 12:18 also speaks to the power of words: "The words of the reckless pierce like swords, but the tongue of the wise brings healing."

God's directive is plain and sobering. James 1:26 sums it up: "Those who consider themselves religious and yet do not keep a tight rein on their tongues deceive themselves, and their religion is worthless."

Ouch!

THE HEART

God's wisdom must also change your heart. Proverbs 2:10 says, "For wisdom will enter your heart, and knowledge will be pleasant to your soul."

God's wisdom will give you love for others. I often ask God to help me care for people when irritation harbors in my heart. Most times, God blesses me three-fold after this request. He provides his wisdom to understand their behavior; he gives me a new attitude about them; and finally, he pours into me his abundant love for them.

HANDS AND FEET

Remember *kok-maw*, the Hebrew word for wisdom, mentioned earlier. It means to be wise in thought and deed. Contrary to our vision, wise people do not sit in a room thinking and spouting off their knowledge. That's not what Jesus did. Wisdom in action has much to do with the working of our hands and feet. In Matthew 11:19, it says, "The Son of Man came eating and drinking, and they say, "Here is a glutton and a drunkard, a friend of tax collectors and sinners." But wisdom is proved right by her deeds. Jesus proved his wisdom by his actions.

God's full vision of wisdom is us having eyes that perceive, ears that really listen, a tongue under control, his love for others in our hearts, and carrying our wisdom into action.

We know Albert Einstein was intelligent, but who, then, is wise? Anyone who fears the Lord, seeks his wisdom, and lets God's wisdom create profound change in her life. Israel's King Solomon, with his 3,000 proverbs, possessed wisdom. A parent whose feet are firmly planted in the way of the Lord is grounded in wisdom. A missionary who understands God's love and lives it out in a harsh and distant land represents the hands and feet of wisdom. The big question is, do you think you are wise? If not, have you asked God for his wisdom? Do you cry out for it, seeking it for the treasure it is—more valuable than silver and gold?

Gloves of Prayer: Lord, like Solomon, I seek your wisdom. Help me to fill myself with your wisdom daily as I learn to trust in you. Prompt me to stay in your Word, for when I open it I receive great treasures of your wisdom. Increase my wisdom as I learn to lean on you and not my own understanding. Open my ears, help me see, change my heart, and let me be a vessel of your active, loving wisdom. In Jesus' name, AMEN.

Discussion Questions:
If I Only Had . . . A Brain

1. Do you believe "If I Only Had . . . A Brain" you would be more secure?

2. Joan considered herself the "dumb kid" because of her hearing issue. Can you relate to her story of feeling dumb? Has Satan ever tried to use this label to keep you from reaching your God-given potential?

3. God has made us all unique. Some of us are artistically intelligent, some of us never forget a face, some of us have athletic smarts. Reflect on the ways in which God has made you intelligent, and make a list of your God-given abilities. Thank him for these gifts.

4. Wisdom begins with knowing what is right according to God and using his perspective to bless others. Wisdom does not always come with age but when we are in relationship with God, he teaches us his truths daily. How has God increased your wisdom over the years?

5. God spoke to Solomon one night as he lay in a restless sleep, "Ask! What shall I give you?" Solomon asked for a discerning heart to govern well. He wanted wisdom. What would you request from God if he asked you the same question?

6. Proverbs 8:11 says, "for wisdom is more precious than rubies, and nothing you desire can compare with her." How valuable is wisdom to you? Do you pursue wisdom like "silver and treasure"? If not, what do you pursue with that degree of passion?

7. Many of us waste our time instead of seeking God's wisdom. What do you do to increase your wisdom? Do you make choices with your free time that increase or decrease your wisdom? Make a plan to take a small step towards acquiring more of God's wisdom.

8. In the end, Solomon stopped pursuing God's wisdom and started pursuing pleasures of the flesh. He lost his wisdom when he stopped walking in relationship with God. Have you ever lost wisdom or stepped away from wisdom when you stepped away from God?

9. Wisdom will sharpen our eyes and ears, make our mouths gentler, and fill our hearts with more love. How has your relationship with God helped you see people differently, control your tongue, and love others more selflessly?

10. The word for wisdom in Hebrew, *kok-maw*, means to be wise in thought and deed. Have you ever thought of wisdom as an action verb? How might doing so change your view of wisdom?

Six

If I Only Had . . .
A Normal Family

A BABY BIRD FELL out of his nest and feverishly searched for its mother. "Are you my mother?" he asked the kitten. In the famous children's book by P.D. Eastman, *Are You My Mother?*, the little robin asks each animal the same question, becoming increasingly desperate as the animals one-by-one answered no.[1] Can you relate to the baby bird in this story? Was there a parent missing from your life? Did you wonder when looking at your parents, *Are you my mother? Are you really my father?* Did you long for someone to be a mother or father to you, to instruct you in those things mothers and fathers are supposed to teach? Are you still looking for someone to be your mother or your father?

I identify with the little bird frantically searching for his mother. Because my own mother never recovered from the premature death of my father, I always looked for someone to fill the family void in my life. On my own during much of my childhood, I learned about the world through trial and error. I realize now my mother's vodka-and-prescription-drugs cocktail was the reason she was somewhat catatonic and unable to engage with me. She gave up drinking in my later elementary years, but my life was still a lot like the movie

Groundhog Day, in which main character Bill Murray wakes up to the same scenario day after day. When I arrived home from school, I usually found my mother sitting in the same chair, smiling the same blank smile at me, stirring her iced tea over and over.

"I got my report card today, mom," I'd tell her. "All A's and B's."

She'd respond with an emotionless, "That's good, Lisa."

Nothing excited my mother, not even my organizing a girl's basketball team in high school or our subsequent tie for the district championship during my senior year. My mother never attended any of my games until my grandfather took her to one of my college basketball games. No excitement about my grades or mother-daughter talks about the birds and the bees. No shopping trips or cooking lessons, no pep talks about life, no support of my extracurricular activities.

I would be lying if I said my mother's behavior didn't affect me. I became a high-achiever and feared being like my mother. Even after I gave birth to two boys, I worked full-time, allowing nannies to care for the children because I did not want to sit home catatonic like my mother. To this day, I have a difficult time being home unless I have something to do. I had to learn on my own how to be domestic because I wasn't taught. When I left full-time employment in 2004, it was a huge leap for me, but I had seminary to keep me busy. I did not have to worry that I would sit in a chair all day, every day, stirring my tea. Do you worry about being just like your mother? What about your father?

Christine's mom and dad were divorced, and for most of her life, her father lived seven hours away. For ten years, she saw him once a year, and sometimes less. Florence remembered coming home from school to her mother's warnings. "Your dad is very angry. It's going to be a long night." Winona called her parents "the bystanders" because they were outside observers to her life. Theresa and her brother were the product of their mother's adulterous affair. For most of their childhood, they lived with their mother and her husband, but snuck out with their mother on weekends to spend time with the man who was their biological father.

Looking at these examples, we know that dysfunction occurs in every family, and it's a bit different in each case. Families are composed of flawed human beings, and there is no way a group of imperfect people can get along perfectly.

Scarf of Truth:
Dysfunction happens in the best of families.

The Bible itself spills over with stories of family dysfunction: Cain and Abel, two brothers whose lives were destroyed by jealousy and murder; Hagar, Sarah's slave, who bore Abraham his first son; and Esau, who sold his birthright to Jacob for a mess of pottage. But one of the best known examples appears in 2 Samuel 11:1–5:

> In the spring, at the time when kings go off to war, David sent Joab out with the king's men and the whole Israelite army. They destroyed the Ammonites and besieged Rabbah. But David remained in Jerusalem.
>
> One evening David got up from his bed and walked around on the roof of the palace. From the roof he saw a woman bathing. The woman was very beautiful, and David sent someone to find out about her. The man said, "She is Bathsheba, the daughter of Eliam and the wife of Uriah the Hittite." Then David sent messengers to get her. She came to him, and he slept with her. (Now she was purifying herself from her monthly uncleanness.) Then she went back home. The woman conceived and sent word to David, saying, "I am pregnant."

King David, the mighty warrior known as a man after God's own heart, gave in to the lust of the flesh and committed adultery. To add to his sin, once he learned Bathsheba was pregnant, he had her husband, Uriah, sent to the front lines to die in battle and took Bathsheba as his wife. What began as a momentary weakness resulted in a lifetime of struggle. David's family life was never the same. The dysfunction broke loose, and not even David's mighty army could corral it.

You may come from one of those families where everything appeared normal on the outside, but behind closed doors, chaos, not peace, was the norm. I remember a nicely dressed woman from my church who seemed to have it all together. She carried herself with poise and confidence, and you would think she grew up in a privileged household. One day, I complimented her about her confidence.

"Things are not always what they seem," she replied. She then told me her story of abuse in her home. She ran away from home at age sixteen and lived in her car until she could get on her feet. She was the last person I expected to have an awful chapter in her life story.

Scarf of Truth:
The sins of parents always affect their children.

This doesn't seem very positive, does it? The point is, if your parents hung out in the muck of sin, some of it rubbed off on you. So be aware of how it might be affecting you, and know you can do something about it!

In David's case, after the prophet Nathan explained to David the gravity of his sin, the consequences began. The baby he conceived with Bathsheba died. His household was disrupted as his son, Amnon, raped his half-sister, Tamar. Then David's other son, Absalom, in an effort to avenge Tamar, had Amnon killed. Because Tamar had been violated sexually, she lived in isolation for the rest of her life. Absalom became estranged from his father, and later, unsuccessfully tried to overthrow his father's kingdom first by having sexual relations with his father's concubines, and then by planning to attack David's kingdom through military force.

Sounds like the perfect storyline for a new soap opera called *As the Bible Turns*. So what did David do to correct the wrong that triggered the avalanche in his family?

Nothing.

He tried to sweep the family improprieties under the Persian rug. His kingdom was eventually safe, but only due to another tragedy that resulted from David's refusal to deal with sin. Absalom, his son-turned-enemy, was on his way to an unfriendly family reunion to stage a coup when a freak accident occurred. A tree branch snagged Absalom's head, but his mule didn't stop, leaving Absalom hanging in midair. If only David had addressed the previous family problems, Absalom wouldn't have been out to get his dad and might not have died so tragically. What a trail of dysfunction and unnecessary death was paved by David's sin of adultery.

Scarf of Truth:
Time does not heal all wounds. We must face our family issues.

David knew all of this was going on in his family, but he did not confront it. He was an absentee dad. In King David's case, if he had taken the blindfold off his eyes, his family history would be recorded as an example of what to do, rather than what not to do. The enmity between his sons might have dissolved, untimely deaths would have been avoided, and Tamar, the innocent victim in this tragedy, could have had a shot at healing. We must face our family issues because if we don't, the fallout can be irreversible. We cannot sweep them under the rug or pretend they did not happen. So how do we deal with our fractured families and let God bring us to a better place?

HEALING BEGINS WITH YOU

In John 5, before Jesus healed the man who had been paralyzed for thirty-eight years, Jesus asked him if he wanted to get well. Rather than respond with a simple yes, the man complained (verse 7): "I have no one to help me into the pool when the water is stirred. While I am trying to get in, someone else goes down ahead of me."

In verse 8, Jesus commanded him to take action: "Get up! Pick up your mat and walk."

This time, the disabled man was cured and picked up his mat and walked. In order to be healed from the past, we have to quit making excuses and take the first step toward healing.

Your healing doesn't depend on your mother or your father getting help. Not even your messed-up uncle or siblings have to heal first. You don't have to wait on anyone else to start the process. Often, parents aren't the mom and dad we dream about. You may never get the apology, the, "I love you," or the bear hug your heart desires. You can sit there waiting for them to change, but it may never happen. The only one you can change is yourself.

You can face family issues by taking action, whether by joining a support group to meet others who are dealing with similar problems, or by finding reading material that addresses recovery and healing. You can form a small group with other people who are committed to open, honest sharing. I participate in a personal intercessory team with three other women. We pray together and share issues we are dealing with so we can pray over them and counsel each other.

I also take part in a spiritual accountability group. Twice a month, we discuss how we are staying connected to the Lord through our reading or action, and pray for the members of our group. You can simply ask a few friends to have a standing lunch or breakfast time where you can talk about your struggles. It is important that you have one or two trustworthy friends who know your story and with whom you can be totally transparent.

BRING THE PAST INTO THE LIGHT

Ephesians 5:11 says, "Have nothing to do with the fruitless deeds of darkness, but rather expose them."

It is imperative not to leave the family dysfunction buried, because eventually, whatever lies deeply buried in your past will erupt in unhealthy ways. I remember my sixty-year-old minister getting up in front of our church one day to share his story. "There is one shadowy corner of my life that I have not allowed God's grace to touch," he said, his hands shaking. "A secret I have protected for years." During all that time he had believed that if he didn't keep quiet about the sexual molestation in his past, his world would fall apart. He finally allowed God's light to shine on that aspect of his life, and his healing began.

Shannon, a beautiful blonde athletic woman, had a similar experience with locking a secret away for years. Her childhood was ripped from her at age five when a family member began sexually molesting her. "I immediately developed an eating disorder because he bribed me with food," she explained. "He threatened me, saying my mom wouldn't love me anymore if I told her this was happening." Since Shannon's biological father and mother were divorced, she had abandonment issues and feared his threat would come true if she told. So for seven years, the abuse raged on. By the time Shannon graduated from high school, weighing 200 pounds, she didn't know what love was or whom she could trust.

For years Shannon's life went up and down like a roller-coaster. She took drugs, got into an abusive relationship, and struggled with an eating disorder. God kept trying to lead her away from anesthetization toward healing. She remembered the time she looked up a drug dealer's phone number in the phone book. "I saw a big ad for Charter Hospital and its program to help people with eating disorders. I decided to go to the hospital and talk to someone. A nurse looked at me and asked, "Have you ever been molested?"

It hit me hard because I had said I was never going to let the molestation affect me. She said, 'Honey, you are dying inside. You have to tell someone.'"

That's when Shannon found courage to tell her story to both her mother and stepmother. When her mother and stepmother found out, they held her and cried. By allowing light into that dark cavern of her life, Shannon's healing process began. She grows stronger each day through Christian counseling and by sharing her story with others who might be dealing with similar issues.

FORGIVE THE FAMILY MEMBERS WHO HURT YOU

Matthew 6:14–16 says, "For if you forgive other people when they sin against you, your heavenly Father will also forgive you. But if you do not forgive others their sins, your Father will not forgive your sins."

Holding onto resentment and anger because of your fractured family can be unhealthy. After I rededicated my life to Christ, I felt a call from God to move back to my home town to honor my mother. At the time, the president of ESPN had offered me a full-time reporting job. It was a job I would have grabbed prior to my rededication to Christ, but I felt the Holy Spirit's tug to make things right with my mother. For years, I had run from her. For years, I feared being like her. For years, I did not have much contact with her, and let other family members deal with her when she strayed off her medication and had to be hospitalized. Now it was time to forgive my mother, honor her, and be the one to take care of her. I turned down the dream job at ESPN and moved back to my home town.

Honoring my mother meant visiting her on a regular basis. At this point, she was unable to live by herself, so she resided in a group home. I gave her money if she needed it and bought her clothes when she asked for them. I brought her grandson over to visit her. For about two years, I gave my mother unconditional love, never expecting anything in return.

One day, my mother told me she needed some shoes. I didn't

know why, but I felt an urgency about it and ran out during my lunch break to find her a pair. It was apparent the Lord was letting me know that time was short, because before I could get the shoes to my mother, I received a call from her caretaker at the group home. She had suffered a massive heart attack and was being rushed to the hospital.

The prognosis was terminal. My mother lay comatose for a week before she died. In that week of waiting, I spent every waking moment at her bedside, telling her I loved her, stroking her hair, just watching her breathe—something I no longer took for granted. She passed quietly in the middle of the night. I am sad that I wasn't at the hospital when she died; maybe God knew I could not handle it.

While I didn't get her new shoes to her in time, I made sure my mother wore them on her earthly shell before it went to its final resting place. My mom, who endured a lifelong struggle with mental illness, was finally healed and at peace in the arms of the Lord. Our relationship was healed, as well; I no longer ran from her or the memories of her. I came to the point where I deeply cared for her, even though she was unable to reciprocate. After my mother passed away, I heard the Lord whisper to me.

"Now you understand what my love is all about."

Forgiveness is a critical step in the healing process.

BE PREPARED FOR HEALING TO TAKE TIME

In our fast-paced world, we want everything at the snap of our fingers. Our microwavable food is ready in one minute. Through text messages, we can reach people immediately. With the invention of the DVR, we no longer have to wait to see what happens next on our favorite television show.

Recovering from the fractured family doesn't work that way. Psalm 90:4 says, "A thousand years in your sight are like a day that has just gone by, or like a watch in the night."

God wants to heal us, but healing our hearts is not like defrosting chicken. Psychologists say a woman or man who was the victim of incest as a child must not only deal with the hurt, anger, and betrayal, but must also totally restructure his or her self-image. They add that healing is not something that can be rushed.

Become a Student of What Is Right

To expose what is wrong in a relationship, you have to know what is right. Psalm 145:4 says, "One generation commends your works to another, they tell of your mighty acts."

You need to find someone who lives according to God's Word and spend time with them. It is difficult to know what is "normal" when you come from a dysfunctional family. If all you know is sexual abuse, like Shannon, how do you know how to have a normal family relationship or enjoy lovemaking as a positive in a marriage relationship?

My grandmother and grandfather argued 24–7. If all you saw growing up was verbal abuse or bickering, how do you expect to understand how to resolve conflict? As a mother, how do you emotionally connect with your husband and children if you never experienced sharing feelings in a healthy relationship with your own father or mother?

A Christian mentor is absolutely essential in discerning what is right and what is not. Do you have an older friend who acts as a parent in your life? For me, it was the mother of the high-school friend who led me to Christ and took me to church every Sunday with her family. Interestingly, I hung out with my friend's mom all afternoon, not my friend. Desperate to find normalcy in a family and a mother figure to guide me, I spent every Sunday afternoon at her feet, studying what a normal, godly mother looked like.

If you don't have a mentor figure in your life and need someone to talk to, some churches have a fabulous Stephen Ministry where a caring church member spends time with you to help you work through any issue you are struggling with. Stephen Ministers are trained to be a good listener and Christian sister or brother to anyone who needs their help.

BE CONFIDENT THAT YOU CAN BE HEALED FROM THE PAST

Hebrews 11:1 says: "Now faith is confidence in what we hope for and assurance about what we do not see."

If you have a mountain to climb, develop the attitude that with God's strength, you will find a way to scale it. Perseverance pays off when you set your mind toward getting emotionally well and doing all you can to help your family do the same. I embraced my family dysfunction as a part of my personal testimony. Can you do the same?

I also see the experiences I endured as gifts from God so I can counsel other people. Can you learn to take all the negatives and look at them in a positive light? I eventually realized that my mother did the best she could while I was growing up; her mental illness got worse after I left for college. Is the same true of your parents? I am thankful she was never critical of me, like some parents, and I realize that through her passivity, I became very independent at an early age. That independence helped me to be successful in life.

BREAK THE CYCLE IN YOUR OWN LIFE WITH GOD'S HELP

The Israelites wandered in the desert for forty years because they did not believe in the power of God. They kept falling back into the old habits again and again. Dealing with family dysfunction can feel a lot like wandering in the desert. You cannot change the past, but you can learn from your family history by not repeating the cycle of dysfunction you grew up in. To do that, you have to acknowledge that you are not immune to repeating the same behavior, and set up boundaries around your life.

If your family has a history of alcoholism and you feel susceptible to it, don't store alcohol in your home. If you have an addiction to prescription drugs, tell all your doctors about your addiction so they will not unknowingly prescribe an addictive pain medication for you. If you have a parent who could not show love to you, then make it a habit in your own family to shower your own children with love. If your family was split due to a parent's infidelity, pray for protection over your own marriage, and do not place yourself in compromising positions. Don't make an old boyfriend a Facebook friend, and avoid flirtatious e-mail exchanges with members of the opposite sex. While these actions in themselves are not adulterous, they can open the door to temptation. It is healing to overcome the family dysfunction you grew up in by not repeating the pattern in your own family.

Scarf of Truth:
God works good out of our trials.

Romans 8:28 specifically says, "And we know that in all things God works for the good of those who love him, who have been called according to his purpose."

Have you ever thought about the dysfunction in your childhood and searched for the good that came out of it? I have, and doing so has in fact contributed to my healing. Because I didn't grow up with a father in my life, I don't have any difficulty relating to God as my father. I can honestly say today that if given the choice to have a relationship with my earthly father or my heavenly father, I would choose my heavenly father. I know some women who had a spectacular father relationship, so they have a tough time thinking of God as a dad. God is the only dad I ever knew.

Because my mother was not engaged with me in my childhood, I became a very strong person. For me, it was sink or swim, and I chose to swim. I also had a wonderful relationship with my loving grandmother, who many times stepped in and provided some of the things my mother was unable to give. It was my grandmother who bought a set of tires for me when mine were bald as an eagle's head, and she made sure I had a beautiful dress when I walked down the aisle at my wedding. While I had a modicum of success in my professional life, I have never forgotten my roots, and my history certainly keeps me humble, for I know that any success I have had came from God. Can you see the good that came out of what you experienced, or are you still bitter and angry about what happened to you?

Our God knows what we need. My life struggles gives me some background to help others. It is my desire that you find victory in your own life.

Scarf of Truth:
As we recover from our family dysfunction, God provides new family members through the body of Christ.

When I married my husband, I received a bonus—my mother-in-law, Sally. A strong Christian, Sally immediately embraced me as a daughter and treated me no differently than her biological children. While her life was cut short by cancer, for eight years before the Lord took her home, she taught me about what the love of Christ looks like in God's family. It is my hope I am already modeling what I've learned from her and will have an opportunity to be a "Sally" to my own daughter-in-law one day.

In Matthew 12:50 Jesus says, "For whoever does the will of my Father in heaven is my brother and sister and mother."

As you go about healing, ask yourself whether you have a group of sisters in Christ with whom you share your life. Finding mothers, fathers, sisters, and brothers who are not blood relatives is one way of healing and recovering from family wounds. Isn't it great to know that as Christians, we have an extended family?

The head of this new family is our father, God. We pray this way, but do we allow him to be the parent we need? Our positive, healthy relationship with a perfect God can go a long way toward healing all other relationships. We can only recover from our fractured families with God's strength. We are encouraged to be honest with God, no matter how gnarled our lives. Read Psalms and notice the emotional honesty expressed therein a book of family conversations between God and a deeply loved child.

I found God to be both father and mother to me. He also placed other Christian sisters in my life after my failed attempt to connect with my estranged biological sister. My earthly father married three times. My mother was his third wife. I don't know why his first two marriages failed, but I do know that he and his first wife had a child, my half-sister. She went to live with her mother after my father died, and I grew up not knowing her.

She resided in the northeast; I was down in Texas, so for many years, the physical distance between us made it too difficult to connect. However, in 1990, my career took me to New York City, and I realized I now lived only three hours from my half-sister, so I called her hoping to establish a relationship. I received a cool reception. She told me the day my father died while playing polo, my mother jumped into the ambulance; she, then fourteen years old, was left on the polo field alone. She said she had to have years of counseling to get over that day, and did not want to share her memories of our father with me.

I was heartbroken. However, because my half-sister didn't want anything to do with me, my friends became my sisters. In fact, I realized recently that God gave me other female sister-friends with the same name as my half-sister throughout my life. I also feel I am a very good friend because I don't have siblings to embrace.

Whether we have been wounded by father or mother, sister or brother, we must realize that only God can fill the void in our lives. Members of Alcoholics Anonymous acknowledge this in the Twelve Step Program when they make a decision to turn their will and lives over to the care of God. I realized AA's twelve steps do not apply just to alcohol; they apply to every area of dysfunction that exists in our lives. (AA's website address is located in the Sources section of this book. Look up the twelve steps, and try to put them into action in your life.)[2]

Remember the little bird from the beginning of the chapter? He did eventually find his mother after a friendly steam shovel placed him back in his nest. Just then, the mother bird came back to the tree. "Do you know who I am?" she said to her baby. The baby bird was sure he finally knew who this was. This was a bird, and this was his mother.

While we may never find the perfect mother or father here on earth, we can find healing from our perfect parent in heaven. "Are you my Father?"

God answers, "Yes, child. I've been waiting for you to ask."

Gloves of Prayer: *I praise you, Oh Lord, for you are my Father in Heaven. You save me from a dysfunctional past and fill the void in my heart. I pray for the strength to finally overcome a family history that paralyzes my progress. Help me to bring any hidden darkness to light and work the trials of my past for good. I want to love you, Father, and know that through you all things work together for good. In Jesus' name, AMEN.*

Discussion Questions:
If I Only Had . . . A Normal Family

1. Christine's mom and dad were divorced and for most of her life, her father lived seven hours away. Florence remembered coming home from school to her mother's warnings. "Your dad is very angry. It's going to be a long night." Winona called her parents "the bystanders" because they were outside observers to her life. Like these women, do you believe "If I only had . . . a normal family" you'd be more secure?

2. The sins of parents always affect their children. Which of your parents' sins have affected you? (Note: the purpose of this is for reflection and self-awareness, not to stir up negative feelings.)

3. Things are not always what they seem. What did you think of the statement, "Dysfunction happens in the best of families"? Has experience shown you this is true? Give an example of when you believed someone had it all together until you found out otherwise.

4. Ephesians 5:11 says, "Have nothing to do with the fruitless deeds of darkness, but rather expose them." Why is it important to address the sins of the past? Are there past sins and hurts you have walled off into a shadowy corner? How can bringing the past into the light allow God's grace to touch this corner of your life?

5. In our fast-paced world, we want everything at the snap of our fingers, but healing takes time. Give an example from your life of God's seemingly slow but thorough healing.

6. To bring healing to our family issues this chapter gives the following ways to deal with our fractured families and let God bring us to a better place: healing begins with you, bring the past into the light, forgive the family members who hurt you, be prepared for healing to take time, become a student of what is right, be confident you can be healed from the past, and break the cycle with God's help. Which seems easiest to you? Which seems most difficult?

7. This chapter said, "Healing begins with you." Jesus told the man who had been an invalid for 38 years to "Get up! Pick up your mat and walk." What do you need to do in your own life to rise above family dysfunction and "pick up your mat and walk?"

8. Matthew 6:14 says, "For if you forgive other people when they sin against you, your heavenly Father will also forgive you." Which family members do you need to forgive? How difficult is it to forgive them? Though it seems impossible, how important is it to forgive as Jesus forgives?

9. The Israelites wandered in the desert for forty years because they did not believe in the power of God. They kept falling back into the old habits again and again. Are you wandering in the desert, so to speak? If so, in what ways? What are some practical ways you can break these cycles of dysfunction in your own life?

10. Through marriage, long true friendships, and the Body of Christ, God often blesses individuals with people who become like family. How has God provided other family members for you?

Seven

If I Only Had . . .
A Better Marriage

DOES YOUR PRINCE CHARMING ever act like a toad? Here's a true story of an amphibian-like husband: Once upon a time on New Year's Eve, a group of friends got together for "game night." The game of choice was *Imaginiff,* where in each round, one player is chosen as the "subject" of a question. Jenny stood in the spotlight. Her question was, "If Jenny was a children's story, what would she be?"

"Alice in Wonderland," said a friend.

Another replied, "Peter Pan." Others replied with equally uplifting and affirmative titles.

Everyone had answered except Jenny's husband. Would he say, *Sleeping Beauty?* Or maybe *Beauty and the Beast?* The group turned toward him, waiting for his romantic response.

"If Jenny was a children's story," he said, "she would be . . . *The Old Woman Who Lived in a Shoe.*"

Jenny's face turned from princess-like to snarled and contorted. Silence filled the room as if everyone were under a spell. Jenny's husband shrunk down in his seat and seemed to keep shrinking and shrinking until there was nothing left, except . . . an old man who might need to find a new boot to live in.

If we are honest, sometimes it feels like this is what happens to our marriages. The relationship starts out with a blissful courtship, but sooner or later, hurtful words or actions leave us wondering, *Who is this person I committed my life to? Was I delirious?* It is at this point we look for an answer, and often land squarely on the solution that our man needs some repair work.

Recently, I watched a popular talk show that announced a contest called "Fix My Man." The program addressed various issues that might need "fixin'" like: your ring gets stuck while you're stroking your man's back hair, or maybe your man has two left feet and dropped you on the dance floor. The producers invited viewers to submit their personal fix-my-man stories, and they would try to help. So how does your man need fixin'?

If you've ever made a list of areas needing improvement, either on paper or in your mind, what should happen to that list? Should you post it on the refrigerator? No.

Tell your friends about it? No.

Make sure the children are aware of each item? No.

With a little ceremony, you should take that list and pray it to God, because he alone has the right tools to accomplish the job.

Scarf of Truth:
Only God can fix your man.

When I think of fixing my man, I think of Michelangelo and his master works of marble. "In every block of marble," Michelangelo explained, "I see a statue as plain as though it stood before me, shaped and perfect in attitude and action. I have only to hew away the rough walls that imprison the lovely apparition to reveal it to the other eyes as mine see it."[1]

Let's face it; our men are like those blocks of marble, in more ways than one. Often, when we try to fix them, the whole sculpting process gets messy. Imagine two sculptors, God and us, with two visions working on the same bit of marble. God is patiently chipping away the excess parts to reveal the beautiful work underneath, and we are hurriedly drilling holes or using a jack hammer to finish the job as quickly as possible. The result will look like Swiss cheese instead of what God intended. (Of course, sometimes there are serious issues that require you to pray and also take action. God does not expect us to live with abuse or constant infidelity.)

I was fairly secure in my own marriage until I moved from my home town of San Antonio to a town five hours north. The fact that I was oblivious to much of my marriage was partly why I felt secure. I was so busy with my career and kids, I didn't give much thought to what was going on with my spouse. For quite a stretch of time during my television broadcasting career, I didn't have a clue where my husband was traveling to or with whom he was traveling. That period of time is a blur, and that's not good for a marriage.

When I moved, I attended seminary part-time and was not working outside the home. Early on, girlfriends were few, so I had a lot of husband time. As I drew closer to my husband and studied him for the first time, it was like using a dermatologist's bright light to look at him. I saw the good parts as well as the warts. I obsessed about what I thought needed fixin, but not enough about what God wanted me to do. I tried to do my own sculpture work.

A friend of mine describes marriage insecurity as a force. It is very difficult to shake it, once it grips you. Whatever is stealing your sense of security becomes a blinking light constantly calling for your attention.

It's important to turn your marital insecurity over to God, but it doesn't mean you can't dialogue with the man in your life in a healthy and respectful way about the things that trouble you. It means praying about what God wants you to say and following his lead instead of taking matters into your own mind, churning them around, and spewing them out of your mouth in a fit of frustration.

My husband and I talked through the issues that were bothering me, and he agreed to make some changes. Many of those changes were in the area of how he dealt with the opposite sex. For example, he agreed to avoid one-on-one lunches with a woman when possible. The social lunches were making me insecure. (It didn't help that I was in the middle of a moral theology class around that time working on a case study about how pastors fall into infidelity with church members.)

This is a two-way street, of course. What's good for the gander is good for the goose. I agreed to discontinue one-on-one lunches with the opposite sex, just as I requested of my husband.

Scarf of Truth:
Our spouses will never make us
100 percent secure in our marriages.

It is good if you can talk to your spouse about what makes you insecure. I hope he will be willing to work with you and make some changes, but no person is capable of making you 100 percent secure.

Recently, I had cleaned the entire house before my husband returned home from the office. I'm no Martha Stewart, but I was proud of my work. When my husband arrived, I greeted him at the door and waited for a word of affirmation. I imagined a *Wow, you've worked hard; it looks so clean!*

Instead, his first words were, "What's that wet spot on the floor?" He'd noticed, but not exactly how I wanted him to notice. Your spouse is human. He will do some things that help, and some things that push your insecurity buttons.

As I age, I still worry that I am not pretty enough for my husband, that he'll find someone younger because he is youthful-looking, or that he'll just get bored with me. Part of my insecurity is due to the fact that my family has a history of adultery, so my background increases my insecurity. The other part is that we live in a culture in which this happen too often. Can you relate?

Possibly, the reason God does not allow us to have perfect husbands or perfect marriages is that if our husband always did everything right, then we wouldn't need God.

We shouldn't put our husbands on the throne in our lives. God wants to be the center of our existence, on the throne; to place our husbands there is idol worship. He wants to be our *Ish*, the Hebrew word for husband. Listen to these beautiful words from Isaiah 54:5–8:

> "For your Maker is your husband (ISH)—the Lord Almighty is His name—the Holy One of Israel is your Redeemer; he is called the God of all the earth. The LORD will call you back as if you were a wife deserted and distressed in spirit—a wife who married young, only to be rejected," says your God. "For a brief moment I abandoned you, but with deep compassion I will bring you back. In a surge of anger I hid my face from you for a moment but with everlasting kindness I will have compassion on you," says the LORD your Redeemer.

These words were written about Israel's estranged relationship with God, comparing Israel to a wife whose husband had rejected her, but I believe we can also take these words to heart. God loves us perfectly as no one else can and wants us to cling to him as a wife clings to a husband. That's why I came up with "Seven Reasons God is the Perfect *Ish* (Husband)." (Seven is the number for perfection in the Bible.)

The first reason God is the perfect *Ish*: **God is never too busy for us.**

One of the consistent complaints heard from women is that their husbands don't spend enough time with them. Men's two most common states seem to be working or chilling. Many are also on the road during the week. Others arrive home, have dinner, and then head to their man caves to hibernate. Wives are lonely and need the companionship of their husbands. I don't like what has happened to the family unit in our generation, but until God corrects it, he will be there for you.

God longs for you to get up early in the morning and read his Word. He desires time alone with you in prayer. When you pray, he doesn't say, "Can I call you back? I'm in a meeting." He craves connecting with you throughout the day. Hear the words of Psalm 121:5–8: "The Lord watches over you—the Lord is your shade at your right hand; the sun will not harm you by day, nor the moon by night. The Lord will keep you from all harm—he will watch over your life; the Lord will watch over your coming and going both now and forevermore."

The Lord watches over our lives *forever.* He's eternally never too busy for us.

The second reason God is the perfect husband: **God listens to us**.

A story about God's listening ear revolves around King Hezekiah, one of Judah's good kings. Hezekiah began his reign at the age of twenty-five and remained in power for twenty-nine years during an age of much bloodshed. Attempting to turn his people back to God, he reopened the temple for worship. He restored the use of musical instruments and singing in the worship service. He encouraged all of Israel and Judah to keep the Passover, which had not been observed for years. However, midway through his reign, serious illness struck. We join the story in 2 Kings 20:1–6:

> In those days Hezekiah became ill and was at the point of death. The prophet Isaiah son of Amoz went to him and said, "This is what the LORD says: Put your house in order, because you are going to die; you will not recover."
>
> Hezekiah turned his face to the wall and prayed to the LORD, "Remember, LORD, how I have walked before you faithfully and with

wholehearted devotion and have done what is good in your eyes." And Hezekiah wept bitterly.

Before Isaiah had left the middle court, the word of the LORD came to him: "Go back and tell Hezekiah, the ruler of my people, This is what the LORD, the God of your father David, says: 'I have heard your prayer and seen your tears; I will heal you. On the third day from now you will go up to the temple of the LORD. I will add fifteen years to your life.'"

Did you hear what God told his prophet to tell Hezekiah? "I have heard your prayer and seen your tears." God hears us even when the TV is on, even when we only say it in our hearts, and even when no one else is listening.

My prayer partners and I have seen amazing answers to our supplications—improved marriages, new jobs, clear direction, and healing. We know God pays attention to our requests, and when we connect with him through prayer, our prayers rise up to him like a pleasing aroma. While studying Revelation 5:6–8, this verse struck me concerning prayer:

Then I saw a Lamb, looking as if it had been slain, standing at the center of the throne, encircled by the four living creatures and the elders. The Lamb had seven horns and seven eyes, which are the seven spirits of God sent out into all the earth. He went and took the scroll from the right hand of him who sat on the throne. And when he had taken it, the four living creatures and the twenty-four elders fell down before the Lamb. Each one had a harp and they were holding golden bowls full of incense, which are the prayers of God's people.

The last part of this passage is where I want to direct your focus. In heaven, the twenty-four elders closest to the throne of God held golden bowls of incense containing what? They contained "the prayers of God's people." Some of you might remember how popular incense was in the '70s. It had an intoxicating smell, like our candles today. When I burn my Crème Brulée candle, all is right with the world. That's what our prayers are like to God. They are a pleasing, almost intoxicating aroma. That's how much God loves it when we talk to him. Ladies, God hears our prayers and answers them!

The third reason God is a perfect husband: **God encourages us.**

I admit, one thing I miss about working full-time is praise for a job well done. At one of my old jobs, my boss called me a bulldog because she knew once I got my teeth into a task, I wouldn't let go until it was completed. Many times, that would result in praise or recognition, and I'd feel like I was appreciated for my hard work. Running a household rarely draws the same kind of praise does it?

I never hear, "Wow, my socks were extra white this time! Your devotion to maintain their quality outshines the competition. For your dedication, you won the Best Laundry Service Award!" or, "Our cupboard is amazing thanks to your planning, coordination and shopping savvy."

I need verbal encouragement, and on occasion I do ask God to bring a little encouragement my way. Inevitably, after I pray for an "attagirl," I receive an encouraging note or email. Sometimes, it's a phone call, and I know God prompted the encourager to contact me. Other times, the positive reinforcement simply comes from the Scripture I am reading or a radio broadcast, but there is an awareness that it comes from God. In 1 Peter 3:8–9, Scripture exhorts us to encourage one another: "Finally, all of you, be like-minded, be sympathetic, love one another, be compassionate and humble. Do not repay evil with evil or insult with insult. On the contrary, repay evil with blessing, because to this you were called so that you may inherit a blessing."

God sends others to encourage us!

The fourth reason God is the perfect husband: **God is content with us.**

We may not always be content with the men in our lives, and they may not always be content with us, but isn't it nice to know that God is content with us? And why wouldn't he be? God gave you your personality; he designed you in the womb. This is confirmed in Psalm 139:13–14: "For you created my inmost being; you knit me together in my mother's womb. I praise you because I am fearfully and wonderfully made; your works are wonderful, I know that full well."

God drew us up us exactly how he wanted us to be. If we look just like God created us to be, and God is obviously content with us, then why aren't we content with ourselves?

The fifth reason God is the perfect husband: **God protects us.**

Every morning, my husband and I pray a prayer of protection over our family, because we know we need it. In my lifetime, I have been hit by a car in middle school, flipped over the handlebars of my bicycle and onto my head in high school, involved in a helicopter accident while interning at a television station, and contracted toxic shock syndrome as a young adult. These are just the biggies. I was born on Wednesday. What do they say about Wednesday's child? "Wednesday's child is full of woe." Yep, that pretty much describes me!

Since we began praying for protection over our family, I have witnessed God's incredible protection on more than one occasion.

When my eldest son, Kyle, was a senior in high school, he was involved in a rollover car accident. Kyle told us he remembered a man breaking the windshield and pulling him out of the car. I believe this was God's protection.

Recently, while I traveling down one of our major thoroughfares, I spotted an older gentleman turning into oncoming traffic and heading straight toward me. Because God alerted me to the danger, I was able to avoid him.

God does protect us, if we ask. He is our Knight in Shining Armor. There are many verses about the Lord's protection in the Bible, but this is my favorite, found in Psalm 91:9–14:

> If you say, "The LORD is my refuge," and you make the Most High your dwelling, no harm will overtake you, no disaster will come near your tent. For he will command his angels concerning you to guard you in all your ways; they will lift you up in their hands, so that you will not strike your foot against a stone. You will tread on the lion and the cobra; you will trample the great lion and the serpent. "Because he loves me," says the LORD, "I will rescue him; I will protect him, for he acknowledges my name."

God protects us!

The sixth reason God is a perfect husband: **God loves us.**

Love is a basic human need. According to *Born for Love,* by Maia Szalavitz and Dr. Bruce D. Perry, "In 1945, Spitz compared babies raised in the then-typical sterile American orphanage with those raised in a cold, institutional prison nursery [with their mothers]. . . Thirty-seven percent of the children in the orphanage were dead before they reached age two—whereas none of the infants raised in prison with their mothers died."[2] When we don't get love, we pay a price in health and longevity.

Are you getting enough love? All of us would like to be loved more than we are now. If we are married, we'd like to think our spouses love us enough to die for us, but here's a flash bulletin: Jesus already did. In many ways, the entire Bible is a love letter to us. Listen to this beautiful passage from Romans 5:6–8: "You see, at just the right time, when we were still powerless, Christ died for the ungodly. Very rarely will anyone die for a righteous person, though for a good person someone might possibly dare to die. But God demonstrates his own love for us in this: While we were still sinners, Christ died for us."

Christ died for us, the ultimate act of love by God, so we can spend eternity with him. God is love. He created love. He created intimacy. If you've ever had a mountaintop spiritual experience on a retreat, you've felt that intimacy. Unfortunately, those experiences are further apart than we'd like them, and it isn't because God moved farther away.

The final reason God is the perfect husband: *God will never abandon us.*

Abandonment can be a scary, painful topic. Marriage in our culture is not what it used to be. A University of California study in 1998 reported that twenty-four percent of men and fourteen percent of women had sex outside of their marriage relationship.[3] Today, according to the *Journal of Couple and Relationship Therapy*, approximately fifty percent of married women and sixty percent of married men will have an extramarital affair.[4] With fifty percent of all marriages ending in divorce, it's easy to be insecure about our marriages and worry about abandonment. The stats don't lie! But God gives us a command not to worry, in Matthew 6:34: "Therefore do not worry about tomorrow, for tomorrow will worry about itself. Each day has enough trouble of its own."

So if we are not supposed to worry, what do we do? We must place our security in God and trust that no matter what happens, God will not desert us. This is not an easy task with pain and heartache on the line, but this is ultimately what gives us peace. God has not promised that nothing bad will ever happen to us, but rather that he will be with us through it all. So when you imagine the worst, or the worst just came home with a heart full of burden about his secret life, let God sit in the seat beside you and hold you. God will never abandon you. Claim this verse from Deuteronomy 31:8: "The LORD himself goes before you and will be with you; he will never leave you nor forsake you. Do not be afraid; do not be discouraged."

Jada experienced God being right beside her in times of trouble. During the good days of Jada's marriage, her relationship with

God wasn't close. "We picked up the Bible on Sunday, went to church, came back, put the Bible in its place, and never picked it up until the next Sunday."

Jada was married for seventeen years with three beautiful daughters when her marriage started unraveling. Her husband had switched jobs, and the new people he worked with had very different lifestyles. "The first Christmas party I went to, my jaw dropped when I saw what went on after the CEO left," Jada said. The longer her husband worked for the new company, the more he adapted to the lifestyle of his coworkers. "He had the suburban Cleavers at home alongside this other wild lifestyle where he would be at the clubs until two o'clock in the morning," Jada said. One time after a night out, he lost his wedding band. He confessed he had taken it off to dance with other women.

During this difficult time, Jada reached out to Barb, one of the prayer warriors at her church. Jada noticed something different about Barb: she had peace and grace. "I wanted to be like her," Jada said.

After Jada's husband refused to give up his new lifestyle, Jada knew they would have to divorce.

"Going through a divorce is like being ripped in two," Jada says. I wasn't sleeping, and it was all I could do to hold it together for the girls." But then God started talking to her. The pain, anger, and hurt felt like it was too much, but God told her to *Just be still and know that I am God*, and warned her that *The tongue gives life and death*.

At the time, Jada didn't know these words were in the Bible, but she knew they were words from God to her. "I wasn't arguing back with my husband anymore, and it was only because God was speaking to me. I was praying, studying, and talking to God daily. I asked God to fill me with his Holy Spirit, constantly." It seemed like a slow process, but after a few months, Jada realized she now had the qualities, peace and grace, that she had recognized in Barb. They were gifts from the Holy Spirit.

One day while at the bank, she felt indignant about his waywardness: *The nerve of him not wanting me! I'm beautiful. I'm smart. I have my own business. What man wouldn't want me?* Then it dawned on Jada. *I have a husband. I have God.* When she left the bank, she praised God out loud with, "Lord, thank you!" She was sure everyone wondered about her sanity. But that day it finally hit her that God took care of all of her needs as well as all of her children's needs. She understood that God was, in fact, the perfect husband.

In a televised sermon, Andy Stanley talked about having a "Backpack God."[5] What an image for how we often relate to God. We carry God around in our backpack and only let him out when we need him. "I'll take you on the plane with me, God, because I want your travel mercies, but when I get to the hotel room, I'm leaving you in the backpack."

Andy Stanley didn't mean backpack God as a pleasant image of how we treat God, but I'd like to stretch this a little bit, making a positive out of it, and say, if you ever have to pack that suitcase, or those boxes, you can count on God making the trip with you. He's as close as the pack on your back. I promise. I have found that to be true of all the moves I have made. God will never abandon you!

Think about what you really need and want from a husband. Now realize that God gives us all those things, and more!

So there you have it—seven reasons God is the perfect *Ish* for us. Let's review:

#1 God is never too busy for us.
#2 God listens to us.
#3 God encourages us.
#4 God is content with us.
#5 God protects us.
#6 God loves us.
#7 God will never abandon us.

So when you start feeling insecure about your marital relationship, instead of reaching for the drill to fix your man, reach out to

God and hang onto these truths. Cling to him. Center your thoughts on him and love him as your Forever *Ish*!

Gloves of Prayer: *Lord, I am guilty of putting my husband on a pedestal, in your place. Thank you for providing for me in ways no human husband can. Help me feel your love. I desire to love you with all my heart. When I'm not content with my spouse, I ask that you turn my thoughts toward you rather than fixate on what is wrong in my marriage. I know you will always be my protector and will never leave me as long as I put my faith in you. In Jesus' name, AMEN.*

Discussion Questions:
If I Only Had . . . A Better Marriage

1. "Does your prince charming ever act like a toad?" Do you believe "If I only had . . . a better marriage" you'd be more secure?

2. A popular TV show announced a contest called "Fix My Man." The program portrayed various spouse issues that might need "fixin." If you could enter the contest, which issue pertaining to your spouse or significant other would you submit?

3. The first Scarf of Truth in this chapter is: Only God Can Fix Your Man. Do you believe this and behave as if it's true? How much do you leave the men in your life in God's hands, and how much do you try to help God out with their remodeling projects?

4. God says he wants to be our *Ish*, the Hebrew word for husband. "For your Maker is your husband (ISH)—the Lord Almighty is His name—the Holy One of Israel is your Redeemer; . . ." Have you ever thought about God wanting to be your *Ish*? If not, how might this idea be helpful?

5. God is the perfect husband for the following seven reasons: God is never too busy for us; God listens to us; God encourages us: God is content with us; God protects us; God loves us; God will never abandon us. Which one comforts you the most? Which one do you have most trouble believing? Explain your answers.

6. God desires time alone with you in prayer. What can you do to carve out more time to spend with him in prayer?

7. When we need verbal encouragement, we can ask God to bring a little our way. Do you need encouragement? Can you name a time when the Lord sent someone to you to provide encouragement when you were in a low place?

8. Romans 5:6–8 says, "You see, at just the right time, when we were still powerless, Christ died for the ungodly. Very rarely will anyone die for a righteous person, though for a good person someone might possibly dare to die. But God demonstrates his own love for us in this: While we were still sinners, Christ died for us." Do you believe firmly and absolutely that God love you? List a few ways he has shown you his love.

9. Deuteronomy 31:8 says: "The LORD himself goes before you and will be with you; he will never leave you nor forsake you. Do not be afraid; do not be discouraged." The thought of abandonment is scary for some and a painful memory for others. Do you fear abandonment or wince at the word? Can you trust God's Word and let him bring peace to these troubled emotions?

10. Instead of reaching for the drill to fix your man, reach your hand out to God and hang on to his truths. If you are struggling in your marriage or with singleness, what truth from this chapter will help you the most? How can you practically replace lies stuck in your head with God's truth?

Eight

If I Only Had . . .
A Child

MY AUNT ALICE LOVED selflessly, listened attentively, and dedicated her life to making sick children feel better. She never married or had children, but not because she didn't desire either one. I can recall a conversation in which she pined about a boyfriend she had dated once—a serious relationship that did not work out. Yet, I never sensed bitterness about the path her life traveled.

Attending college in the 1930s, Aunt Alice chose the unusual field of recreational therapy. She believed having fun contributed to healing, so she spent much of her career developing games for sick children in hospitals. Through these games, she showed them compassion and love. Because of her success and dedication, Alice received a commendation award from then-President Dwight W. Eisenhower. When she retired, Aunt Alice still surrounded herself with children, volunteering as a docent at Chicago's Children's Museum.

Beth, the daughter of one of my aunt's friends, said Alice was beautiful and magical. "As a child, I always looked forward to visiting her. She had a pet Myna Bird, Barney, and she was a great storyteller," Beth said. "In fact, I recall her telling a story so well I burst into tears at the scary part, much to her horror! Alice has been one of the greatest role models in my life. She inspired me to work with children, and it is how I ended up in Early Childhood Education. If I can live my life in such a way that little children see me as I saw her, I will consider myself to be successful." While my aunt never bore children, she filled her life by placing herself in the midst of thousands of children, some of whom recovered from serious illness thanks to her attentiveness and care.

Being childless is a choice for some women, but for others, it causes much grief and insecurity. Mother's Day, baby showers, and birth announcements can be a painful reminder of what they want but cannot have. Do you want a girl, but you have a houseful of boys? Do you deeply desire a large family, but have only one child? Have you prayed desperately for a child or for extending your family? Do you wonder whether God hears your prayer and understands your pain?

Scarf of Truth:
God understands barrenness.

Heart-wrenching stories of barren women lace the Bible. The three mothers of the Israelite nation, in fact, all struggled with infertility. Sarah, wife of Abraham; Rebekah, wife of Isaac; and Rachel, wife of Jacob, all longed for children and did not bear them until their later years. Elizabeth, the mother of John the Baptist, was so beyond normal childbearing years that when she became pregnant, her husband questioned Gabriel's pregnancy announcement. He paid the price for his disbelief, unable to utter a word until his son was born. God, in his goodness, filled his Book with many examples of women who felt insecure because of infertility.

Let's turn the history pages back to 900 B.C. and take a closer look at another woman of the Bible who dealt with barrenness. She didn't have the needle-prodding tests, in vitro, or the big doctor bills, but she did have the yearning in her heart and the shame of not being able to fulfill her social role. Being fruitful and multiplying was a woman's reason for existing in ancient cultures, so you can understand Hannah's agony over her inability to bear a child.

Hannah was one of the two wives of Elkanah in a dysfunctional household. Elkanah's wife, Peninnah, had babies. Hannah didn't, and Peninnah liked to hold it over her head. The taunting was so severe year after year that Hannah was driven to tears, and at times couldn't eat because life at home was often unbearable. It didn't matter that her husband, Elkanah, favored her.

Every year, when Elkanah made the trip out of town to worship and sacrifice, he would bring back some choice meat for the family to enjoy. He would give portions to Peninnah and to all of her sons and daughters, but because he loved Hannah more, he would dole out twice as much meat to her. This did not satisfy Hannah, and her husband couldn't understand. So he asks her in 1 Samuel 1:8: "Hannah, why are you weeping? Why don't you eat? Why are you downhearted? Don't I mean more to you than ten sons?"

No one understood. Hannah knew she'd be fulfilled if only she had a baby. Her husband didn't understand the longings of her heart, but God did. Hannah wept, and God saw her tears. Oftentimes we try and camouflage the pain, but there's no hiding the truth from God. He knows the deepest longings of our hearts, and he desires for us to turn, face him, and pour out our soul. Hannah didn't pretend it wasn't painful; she spilled out her sorrow to God. Are we willing to do the same?

Scarf of Truth:
Being barren is not a punishment from God.

When the most famous down-and-out Bible character, Job, went through all his hardships, losing his family, his wealth and his health, he questioned God's goodness and treatment. In Job 31:5–6, we see his inquiry: "If I have walked with falsehood or my foot has hurried after deceit—let God weigh me in honest scales and he will know that I am blameless . . ." Job acted the way we all behave during times of trial. He wondered what he'd done to deserve his troubles.

When we ask *Why me?* and scan our lives, memories of our own sin will always pop up like a blinking marquee. The question then becomes, is *God punishing me? Is my sin too great for God to forgive?*

Let me reassure you that no matter what is in your past, if you have confessed it, God has forgiven you. The Scripture 1 John 1:9 confirms, "If we confess our sins, he is faithful and just and will forgive us our sins and purify us from all unrighteousness."

God is not using infertility as a punishment for anything—not a past abortion, or a promiscuous life, or any sin, big or small.

We only have to look at the parable of the lost son in Luke to understand the vastness of God's forgiveness. In Luke 15:21–24, Jesus shares the story:

"The son said to him, 'Father, I have sinned against heaven and against you. I am no longer worthy to be called your son.'

"But the father said to his servants, 'Quick! Bring the best robe and put it on him. Put a ring on his finger and sandals on his feet. Bring the fattened calf and kill it. Let's have a feast and celebrate. For this son of mine was dead and is alive again; he was lost and is found.' So they began to celebrate."

God is not a God of tit-for-tat. He freely forgives us and blesses us. We may never know why we haven't received the family we desired, but it is not a punishment from God. Can you trust that our Father in heaven is sovereign and acknowledge his greatness?

Scarf of Truth:
God is sovereign.

Alyssa and Chris understand what it's like to trust God's sovereignty even when circumstances stretch their faith. While they have given birth to one child, their attempt to have a second has hit a roadblock, as Alyssa miscarried four times due to a Kell genetic issue. When a mother or father is Kell-positive, there is a fifty-percent chance the baby will also be Kell-positive. The prognosis is not good. The baby develops hemolytic disease, causing the baby's body to kill off its own red blood cells.

Alyssa lost two children in the first trimester and also miscarried two other babies after carrying them twenty weeks. "I don't consider myself barren because I have one child on earth and four in heaven whom I can't wait to meet. I never went through periods of anger at God, mostly just grief, but even then, my mind and my heart knew God is ultimately on the throne. He is sovereign, and it was a matter of trusting his perfect will for me, which was not exactly what I would have chosen, but still good." Alyssa admits there are times when she struggles, when friends around her seem to have no issues having multiple children, but she says she goes back to God's sovereignty. "I don't know yet that God has promised us another child, but I do have the desire, which I believe is from him."

Yes, God is sovereign.

However, in the midst of his suffering, Job challenged God's sovereignty, and God responded strongly with an answer that canvasses four chapters, from Job 38 to 41. Here are a few quotes from His response: "Where were you when I laid the earth's foundation? Tell me, if you understand. Who marked off its dimensions? Surely you know! Who stretched a measuring line across it? On what were its footings set, or who laid its cornerstone while the morning stars sang together and all the angels shouted for joy?" (Job 38:4–7) God apparently made his point, because at the end of his soliloquy, Job had a brief response compared to his other complaints: "Then Job replied to the LORD: 'I know that you can do all things; no purpose of yours can be thwarted. You asked, 'Who is this that obscures my plans without knowledge?' Surely I spoke of things I did not understand, things too wonderful for me to know.'" (Job 42:1–3)

While Job could not see past his hardships, God eventually restored Job's life, showering him with more than he ever possessed before. We may never understand why on this side of the pearly gates, but we can cling to trust, instead, and count on God's sovereignty.

Scarf of Truth:
Security is a fruit of accepting God's plan for your life.

Even though Hannah was extremely distraught about her barrenness, she was secure that God had a plan for her life and knew that only he could provide a child. One day, she prayed outside the temple, weeping bitterly, saying in 1 Samuel 1:11: "LORD Almighty, if you will only look on your servant's misery and remember me, and not forget your servant but give her a son, then I will give him to the LORD for all the days of his life, and no razor will ever be used on his head."

Eli the priest stood nearby, and thought Hannah was drunk because her lips were moving, but he couldn't hear her voice. No, Hannah hadn't stopped at the liquor store on her way to church. She was pouring out her soul to the Lord: "Do not take your servant for a wicked woman; I have been praying here out of my great anguish and grief." (1 Samuel 1:16)

Like Hannah, Fay was troubled and frustrated. She grew up in the '50s when every girl's dream was to get married and have a family. "I went to college and started my teaching career after I graduated, but as for getting married, it just wasn't happening," Fay said. "I was a bridesmaid five times in one year."

As she approached thirty, panic set in.

One night she fell to her knees and prayed. "Dear God, I have so much love in my heart, and I want to share it with others, but if marriage and having kids is not the path you chose for me, I need to know your direction."

A week after Fay's prayer, she met Fred at a broom hockey party. He was the goalie. "We started talking, and suddenly we were friends. I knew there was something special about him, but we were both dating other people."

Six months later, Fay ran into Fred at a pig roast. It was then she found out he was divorced, with four boys. "We dated a little bit, and by the time January rolled around, the relationship was getting more serious. By March, we were engaged, and we were married in August." She went from being a single teacher to being a wife and step-mom of four boys.

Fay and Fred did try to conceive a child, but their attempts never resulted in a baby. Years later, Fay realized that even though she never gave birth to children, God always blessed her with children, and she was secure in the plan he had laid out for her. As a teacher and administrator, she "mothered" students for thirty-five years. As a woman who married a man with four children, she was also a mother to their four boys, and now, as a grandmother, she has the opportunity to love on children again. "On Mother's Day, I get four phone calls," Fay said of her now-grown young men. "They call for advice for stuff, and one of the boys, Chad, would also tell you I was instrumental in his coming to Christ."

"God hears your heart," Fay said. "I always say about my wedding day, I am sure people were looking at me and thinking I was either crazy, or crazy in love. I know it was a God thing as much for Fred as it was for me."

Fay and Fred have been married for over 30 years. "We were brought together by God and continue to trust in his plan for us.

The plan God had for me was certainly not anything I could ever have imagined. But it has strengthened me and taught me to have faith in him," Fay said.

God has a plan for our lives, but it may not be the one we envisioned. After God told Abraham and Sarah they would have a baby late in life, Sarah didn't totally buy into God's program. She tried to speed up the process by lending Abraham her maid servant, Hagar, to bear a child for them. Her lack of faith resulted in family division and resentment as well as cruelty toward Hagar and the son she bore, Ishmael. Down the road, Sarah did give birth to her own child, Isaac, just as God had said. If only she had accepted God's promise to her without diverting from it.

My life verse is Jeremiah 29:11: "For I know the plans I have for you, declares the Lord, plans to prosper you and not to harm you, plans to give you hope and a future." Whenever I question or worry about a situation in my life, I retrieve my life verse and repeat it to myself again. I think, *I know this is no fun right now, but God's desire is to prosper me and not to hurt me. He gives me my hope, and he has my future laid out for me.* If you are barren or unable to have as many children as you would like, remember Jeremiah 29:11, and trust that God wants the best for you. Know that his plan is already in place, and it is perfect.

Scarf of Truth:
Oftentimes, God answers our prayers for a child.

After Hannah prayed for a child, Scripture said "her face was no longer downcast" (1 Samuel 1:18). Despite her barren womb, she knew God could provide a child— and he did. Once she bore her son Samuel, as an act of gratitude, Hannah gave him back to the Lord so he could serve as a priest for the rest of his life. Samuel became the distinguished final judge of Israel, anointing both Saul and David as king. When God blessed Hannah with a child, she praised his attributes in a poem in 1 Samuel 2:1–2,5: "My heart rejoices in the Lord; in the Lord my horn is lifted high. My mouth boasts over my enemies, for I delight in your deliverance. There is no one holy like the Lord; there is no one besides you; there is no Rock like our God ... She who was barren has borne seven children, but she who has had many sons pines away."

When Hannah received the gift of a child, she realized God was the giver of the gift. Instead of being bitter over all she endured, she was joyful. According to the MacArthur Bible Commentary, the prominent idea in Hannah's prayer is that the Lord is a righteous judge. "He had brought down the proud (Peninnah) and exalted the humble (Hannah)."[1] While God answered Hannah's prayer for a child, she also knew that if he chose not to, he was God, and it was his prerogative to do as he saw fit. While the Lord does not always open the barren womb, Hannah did give birth to five more children after Samuel. However, because she acknowledged God's sovereignty in her life, I have to believe if Samuel had been an only child, he would have been enough for Hannah.

Scarf of Truth:
Let God open your heart to his possibilities.

Drowning in our heartbreak, we often get stuck on what we want. Dreams of what our families will look like occupied our minds even when we were young girls: two kids, maybe three, a daughter to dress up, topped off with a pink bow in her hair, a broad-shouldered son who takes after our handsome husband. ... We imagine how the story should unfold, and when it doesn't, we grieve for that loss. Our dream life didn't happen.

After we cry out, we then have a choice. We can nail ourselves to that dream or we can lay our dream at the base of the cross and allow God to open our hearts and mind to his possibilities. At the base of our dream to have children is a deep desire to love someone. We know there is no shortage of people to love; there is an abundance of children to nurture. There is no scarcity of children who need mothers, either in the literal sense or as mother figures. Can you allow God to open your heart to his vision of the mother he wants you to be?

Penny and her husband, Chip, married when Penny was thirty-six. The two wanted a family, and because of Penny's age they began trying to conceive right away. Nothing happened. By the time Penny turned thirty-nine, the couple was using fertility drugs and shots. Penny remembered the craziness of the process.

"It didn't matter where we were when it was time for a shot," she said.

One time, a shot came due while they were staying at the one-hundred-year-old lodge in Yellowstone National Park. She had a black circle drawn on her back over each hip to help her husband know where to administer the shot. This time, as her husband inserted the needle, a stream of blood shot across the room like Old Faithful. "We hurried around trying to clean up the blood so it wouldn't look like a crime scene!" Penny said.

"Women are supposed to get pregnant, but it didn't happen, and everyone around me was having children," Penny said. She was a teacher during this time and missed many days of school to undergo fertility treatment. "I prayed a lot about it because the situation was spiraling out of control. I wore a necklace with a charm on it that said 'Let go; let God.' Every time I thought about it, I would touch it. I didn't take it off for two years. The charm reminded me that if God didn't intend for me to be pregnant, that's just the way it was."

Penny remembered the Sunday night family dinner with her in-laws when she and her husband delivered the big news. "We have decided to adopt," she said.

My sister-in-law burst into tears the moment the words left my mouth.

She explained through sobs that she was so happy because she was pregnant and hadn't told us for a couple of months. She didn't want to add to our frustration by being one more person who could easily get pregnant.

Penny and Chip know beyond a shadow of a doubt that God's hand was in the adoption. "The sister of a lady I worked with owned a restaurant in a different town. The eighteen-year-old daughter of a woman who was employed there was pregnant and did not want to keep the baby. We took her to the Methodist Mission Home in San Antonio, Texas, where we signed paperwork to make the adoption official. We were in the delivery room with her when Jake was born."

Years later, God orchestrated events to bring a second baby into their life. Their paperwork was in, and they'd been waiting a long time for their second adoption. They decided they were okay with one child, and made the decision to wait until the end of March. If they didn't have a baby by then, they'd stop the adoption process. "The phone rings, of course, on March nineteenth," Penny said, "with a call that they had a baby for us. It was never the way we planned it, but these are my children." Anyone who sees Penny walking with her two sons is amazed by the resemblance they have to each other and to their mother. People clearly see God's handiwork in bringing these two boys and their parents together into a forever family.

Penny and Chip, like many adoptive parents, feel that although their children were born to other parents, God moved mountains to bring them together. Somewhere out there a child longs for a family. If that is God's plan for you, he will help you make it a reality.

Scarf of Truth:
Follow God's call to be a spiritual mother.

No one posts an ad in the paper: "Wanted—Spiritual Mother," but many women have a deep and compelling need for spiritual direction from another female. In Titus 2:4–5, Paul encourages women to direct each other: "Then they [the older woman] can urge the younger women to love their husbands and children, to be self-controlled and pure, to be busy at home, to be kind, and to be subject to their husbands, so that no one will malign the word of God."

If you are interested in the job, spiritual mothers can lead women to Christ, help them walk closer to him, model Christian living, and provide spiritual counseling. When I managed a public relations staff, any time we had a job opening on my staff, I'd pray the Lord would draw someone to the job that I could mentor. One day, a pretty, young blonde dropped into our office to ask if we had an available position. We did, and I asked God, "Is this the one?"

As it turned out, Lara did apply, and she landed the job. The circumstances for Lara moving from California back to Texas were unfortunate. After a long battle with cancer, her mother was dying, and Lara had returned to care for her.

During the time she worked for me, I had opportunities to share my faith with Lara, who was not a Christ-follower at the time. I sponsored her on a spiritual retreat, where she felt the power of the risen Christ and accepted him as her Lord and Savior. During the course of her mother's illness, as well as after her mother died, I considered myself Lara's "spiritual mother." Even after she and I moved to other cities, I'd call Lara when I felt a tap on my shoulder from the Holy Spirit to check on her. When she answered, she'd say, "I can't believe your timing! You must have known I needed to talk to you."

Now, after PR stints in Chicago and the New York City area, Lara landed another job in my area and works thirty minutes away, so we are able to see each other regularly. I don't think it's a coincidence she and I are in closer proximity at this time. As she one day moves into marriage and possible motherhood, I think God has placed me in her life to be a mother to her, whether it be to give her dating advice, or to one day help her pick out her wedding dress!

In 3 John 1:4, John talks about his spiritual children: "I have no greater joy than to hear that my children are walking in the truth."

I agree with John. I am proud of my spiritual children, and I love the role of spiritual mom. It has eternal rewards.

Scarf of Truth:
We learn from God during the barren times.

It's in the desert stretches of my life that I've drawn the closest to God and made the most spiritual progress. I remember one desolate period when someone close to me had, in my opinion, betrayed me. I shared my heartbreak with a fellow seminary student.

She replied, "Have you asked God what he wants you to learn from this?"

I hadn't, because I was too busy feeling sorry for myself and asking God why he allowed the troubles. When I emerged on the other side of my wasteland, I realized I had to go through this barren period of my life in order to live in a more fertile land. Through the trial, my prayer life improved. I became more immersed in God's Word as I sought his answers for my situation, and I realized that although I cared deeply for the person who had hurt me, only God could provide the security I needed. This was the fruit that grew out of a barren time.

Issues of infertility can have polar opposite affects. On one hand, they can cause us to turn our backs on God in anger and doubt. On the other hand, they can cause us to draw closer to him for comfort and love.

Kris chose to draw nearer to God as she prayed Psalm 113:9 over her life repeatedly: "He settles the childless woman in her home as a happy mother of children." Kris desperately wanted a baby, but could not conceive, even though testing couldn't find the crux of the problem.

"When we moved to a new town in 1978, I went to a very small Lutheran church by myself one Sunday. I had grown up in the Lutheran church but had been attending other churches. The church was in a temporary building and very noisy with people visiting with each other. I wasn't sure I would go back again, but I decided to sign the guest book when I left. That was in October. In November, I received the church newsletter in the mail. One of the headlines really caught my eye: 'Anyone interested in adopting?' It was from Lutheran Social Services, informing people of a group meeting for potential adoptive parents."

Kris and her husband signed up and attended the meeting. One hundred twenty-five couples showed up, and Kris and her husband were one of the twenty-six couples accepted for further study. Nine months later, they were blessed with a perfect one-week-old son. Kris knows her prayers were heard by God. "Do I think it was a coincidence that I went to that church and decided to sign the guest book that Sunday? Absolutely not! God's hand was there all the time."

Kris learned they must thank God for his divine plan and that he gives us the faith to wait for his best outcome. God was her teacher during a time of barrenness. We can learn from him, as well, if we ask God to share his lesson plan with us.

No matter where you stand with your infertility struggle, always remember that God loves you and has a heart for you. He understands your needs and will absolutely fill the emptiness in your life. As Christians, we do not walk alone through any heartache or trial.

Jesus assures us in Matthew 11:28-30: "Come to me, all you who are weary and burdened, and I will give you rest. Take my yoke upon you and learn from me, for I am gentle and humble in heart, and you will find rest for your souls. For my yoke is easy and my burden is light."

I recently saw a profound sign that read: JESUS LEFT THE TOMB EMPTY SO YOUR HEART WON'T BE.

God fills our hearts on this journey, but he doesn't always write our story exactly how we planned. I remember a time when a man in my life wasn't responding to me the way I desired, and a friend said, "Why don't you just write a script for him?"

That stung, but it was the truth I needed to hear. We can't write a script for God, but we must believe that even when we are living in the barren land, he desires a happy ending for us. My Aunt Alice found her happiness through working with sick children; Penny and Kris delighted in their adoptions; Fay married into a boisterous family of boys; and Hannah rejoiced at the birth of her six children.

They all saw the truth of God's Word in Philippians 4:19: "And my God will meet all your needs according to the riches of his glory in Christ Jesus."

Gloves of Prayer: *Lord God, I do not understand why I have not been blessed with a child but I know you have a reason for my barrenness. If I am never supposed to have biological children, point me in the direction I should go. Help me to embrace adoption if that is what you want from me, or provide a spiritual son or daughter whom I can teach about you. Lord, show me how to trust you even when you don't provide what I long for so deep within my heart. In Jesus' name, AMEN.*

Discussion Questions:
If I Only Had . . . A Child

1. Do you believe "If I Only Had . . . A Child" you'd be more secure?

2. Have your prayers for a child, or the prayers of someone you know, gone unanswered? Describe the situation. Is it hard to understand why God has not provided a biological child? Even though you do not understand, can you leave the situation in God's arms?

3. Hannah was one of the two wives of Elkanah in a dysfunctional household. Elkanah's wife Peninnah, had babies. Hannah didn't. How can you relate to Hannah? Have you ever prayed for something while God seemed to be blessing everyone around you with what you wanted? A child? A good job? Friends? Explain.

4. Like Hannah in 1 Samuel 1:10–11, are you comfortable pouring out your pain to God? Why or why not?

5. When we ask "Why me?" and examine our lives, memories of past sins will pop up like a blinking marquee. Infertility is painful and might even seem like a punishment from God. Do you ever think God withholds his blessing because of a specific sin in your life? If so, read 1 John 1:9. Confess any sins that need to be confessed and be assured that you are now righteous.

6. In her prayer, Hannah asked for a son and then gave him back to the Lord. For those of us who are parents, this act of dedication reminds us to whom our children ultimately

belong. Is it difficult for you to offer your child(ren) back to God? Why or why not?

7. God has a plan for our lives, but it may not be the one we envisioned. After Abraham and Sarah were told by God they would have a baby late in life, Sarah didn't totally buy into God's program. She tried to speed up the process by lending Abraham her maid servant, Hagar, to bear a child for them. Her lack of faith resulted in family division that has spanned the centuries. Have you ever tried to hurry up a blessing from God, with disastrous results? Explain.

8. Drowning in heartbreak, we often get stuck on what we want. Dreams of what our families should look like occupy our minds. What were your dreams for your life when you were young? What do you envision for your life now? Do you think God has a different vision? Can you ask God to open your heart to possibilities that aren't in line with your vision for your life?

9. In 3 John 1:4, John talks about his spiritual children. Do you have spiritual children? If you are lonely, ask God to bring people to love into your life. Ask God to make you aware of people who need a spiritual mother.

10. It's often during the desert stretches in our lives that we draw the closest to God and make the most spiritual progress. Describe a desert time in your life and what God taught you during this stretch.

Nine

If I Only Had . . .
Closer Friendships

MARTHA STOOD IN FRONT of her glass storm door, gazing out at a group of friends as they jogged by without her.

"Why didn't your running buddies invite you?" her son asked. Martha's throat tightened. This was the third activity this week she hadn't been invited to. *What have I done to lose this whole group of friends?* she wondered. They had worked out together, sat and talked in front of their houses at night, and shared deep concerns about their children. They helped each other through difficult times. Suddenly, the calls and texts had stopped. "I asked God why they didn't want to be friends with me, and at first, I got no answer," Martha said.

As Martha's neighborhood life was falling apart, she received an invitation to be interviewed by a woman from her church. The woman was writing a book and had given her a list of questions, one of which was: "Are you experiencing the love of the Father in a church environment?"

Martha answered truthfully, saying, "I don't have any good friends at my church." After reading Martha's answers, the woman sprang into action and invited her to a few groups at church. As her neighborhood friendships were dissolving, new friendships at church formed.

But Martha still wondered why all her old neighborhood friends were going away. During this time, two of her running buddies, Julie and Emily, became close. Emily had just divorced, and Julie, who was married, was trying to help Emily find a new husband.

Soon, they were going to the bars weekly. "I still had this desire to be liked by them and wanted to be included," said Martha. "Honestly, I felt I wasn't good enough or fun enough for them. I spent too much time asking God why this was happening and crying about how little they cared about me."

One day, Martha finally got the answer to her *why* question when Julie's sad husband broke the news to her at the bus stop. "My wife and I are getting a divorce." By choosing to frequent the bar scene for a friend's sake, Julie had opened the door for her own heart to be led astray. "It wasn't what was wrong with me," Martha said. "I wasn't too slow or not fun enough. It was about which friendships were best for me and what God did not want me involved in." Martha knows now that God ripped those friendships out of her life to protect her from temptations and trouble.

Recently, Martha received confirmation of this at her church small group meeting. "I looked around the room at the smiles of my new friends, and I knew God had blessed me. Yes, he took people out of my life, but he more than abundantly supplied new friends."

There are many famous friendships. Lucy had Ethel; Thelma had Louise; Wilma had Betty; and Astro had George Jetson. Like these well-known examples, most of us realize how important friendships are and know God designed us to connect with each other. Women seem to need friends more than men. Perhaps one of the best songs about the nature of friendship is "Lean on Me," written by Bill Withers. We not only lean on friends, but they also lift us up, share laughter, listen, and hold us during difficult times. But as beautiful as friendships are, they can also be the root of insecurity—and this applies to both existing friendships and those we desire. Have you experienced some of these situations?

- You have a good friend you haven't heard from in weeks. Are you worried she's pulling away because she doesn't like you anymore?
- You move to a new town, and everyone seems connected. No one reaches out to you. Are you concerned you aren't fun enough, rich enough, pretty enough, or smart enough?
- You find out that one of your friends is having lunch with another friend and you weren't invited. Do you agonize about whether they will grow closer and leave you out? Do you wonder if you will be the main course in the lunchtime conversation?
- Everyone raves about one of your dynamic friends. You know she's pretty terrific, but when she's around, are you plagued with concerns about your own likeability?

These scenarios point to insecurity in friendships. So how do we become more secure in our friendships? We need to take the time to learn about friendship from the Bible and also listen to the qualities the people around us consider key for these important relationships. To accomplish this second consideration I conducted an informal friendship poll by asking people via Facebook to share what characteristics they considered to be indicative of a good friend. Of course, I can't tell you whom to befriend or solve your friendship problems. But if you will listen to God's advice, he will help your friendships improve by leaps and bounds. Let's have fun with this one, using an acrostic, FRIEND.

F: (Scarf of Truth)
Forced friendships don't work, and can heighten insecurity.

Let's be honest. It shouldn't be about whom we want to be friends with. It should be about whom God wants in our lives. Some people seem like sparkling jewels to us. Because they are funny and charismatic, we are naturally drawn to them. You want to be the friend of such a person, but only God knows whether it would be a good relationship for you.

When I moved to North Texas after a twelve-year stretch in my home town, I believed that soon my life would overflow with new friends. I was surprised when no one baked cookies for us when we moved in. Trying to befriend neighbors was disappointing because they weren't interested in being friends with me. Even after we found a church home, making friends wasn't easy. I would ask people from our Sunday school class to lunch. They were busy. I would mention to couples that we should have dinner sometime . . . no reaction.

At first, I questioned myself and my appeal, but then I began to pray for God to bring me friends. Do you do that? Pray about friend- ships? It's amazing, but once I began to pray for friends, I made friends without having to force the relationships. If they didn't want to be friends with me, I trusted it wasn't part of God's plan and didn't sulk about it. God prevented that relationship from happen- ing for a reason. If you have prayed for friends, you can rely on him to hand-select them for you!

Martha knows now God will bring you friends when you pray for them, but for a few months, as her old friendships fell apart, she was a little shaky on that concept.

Our best friendship advice comes from the Master. Jesus, in his friendship with the disciples, didn't chase after them. He just said, "Follow me." No pressure. It was their choice. My guess is, if they'd had cell phones and texting back then, Jesus' friends would have been the pushy ones. Imagine the text messages. When the disciples were battling the storm at sea: "Say, BFF, R U There? In boat, going to die! Where R U?"

When Jesus' good friends Mary and Martha notified Jesus of their brother's illness: "Jesus, Lazarus is sick. Come quick! K? M and M."

Just keep in mind that as God starts supplying you with friendships, it's important not to put parameters on those friendships. Recently, God brought a new friend to me, a wonderful encourager, who is seventeen years younger than I am. For a while I resisted this friendship, even though we both had a media background and were both called to Christian motivational speaking and writing. At a retreat we worked at together, I mentioned the age difference one too many times. Eventually, a woman came up to me and said,"Lisa, don't worry that she is younger than you. It's not important. God has brought you together as friends."

Becky, a Midwesterner now living in Texas, had a similar experience. A new woman depicting the stereotypical Texas female walked into her meeting. She had big hair, was all done up, and was hugging and loving on everyone. "I actually had the thought that I could never be friends with her," Becky says. Within two minutes, this same woman shared she suffered from the identical anxiety disorder Becky did. "I could almost hear God laughing," she said. Today, these two women are the best of friends.

R: (Scarf of Truth)
Room: Give friends room to mess up.

In Bible talk, giving friends room to mess up means offering love and grace. Our friends will sometimes disappoint us by forgetting a birthday; at times, they will be crabby and tired, and react with harsh words; other times, they won't be there for us when we need them. In our informal friendship poll, one woman said her closest friends are those who accept her as she is, blemishes and all! Do any of your friends have a wart of prejudice, a freckle of gossip, or a pimple of pride, hating to admit they are wrong? We all want other people to allow for our mess-ups, but do we do the same for them? I have seen many friendships break up when a friend disappoints or hurts another friend's feelings. I've got news for you. Given time, every friend will hurt your feelings.

When the inevitable happens, what do you do? Do you let it go, confront them, nurse the injustice, pull away and clam up, or carry the hurt around for years? I am the type to confront a friend and let her know my feelings are hurt. We all have our ways we typically react to hurt, but giving grace to our friends involves taking the hurt to God first. He can then lead us to the truth about the situation, including our part in the matter. He can show us how our hurt should be dealt with and direct us in the process of healing, which often goes against our learned reactions to pain. Grace will allow you to not let an issue fester, retreat from the friendship, and lose the bond over a misunderstanding. Friendships are worth saving.

Friends will also help us grow up through the giving and receiving of this grace. Proverbs 27:6 speaks to this: *Wounds from a friend can be trusted, but an enemy multiplies kisses.* In other words, it takes a good friend to hold you accountable! Friends are often the only ones who will tell you nicely that your slip is showing, you have a piece of spinach between your teeth, and that some repetitive behavior of yours is hurtful.

Years ago, I got a taste of this from a good friend. Running late for lunch one day, I called her and told her I had to mail a letter at the post office on my way to meet her. Truth be told, I was almost always late. She sought retaliation by leaving the restaurant to run some errands before I arrived. This caused me to sit alone at the restaurant for at least twenty minutes before she returned. I didn't have a clue what was going on. She didn't answer my phone calls, and when she finally arrived, I asked her where she had been.

She answered, "Oh, I went to the bank and the post office . . ."

When I realized she was making a point about the need to be on time, I was upset and began to cry. She felt badly but went on to say that her time is valuable, too. In the end, she forgave me for presuming on her patient nature, and I forgave her for handling her frustration in a way that felt punitive. I was never late for lunch with her again. Some friendships might have broken up over this conflict. She is still a very close friend to this day, and nothing like that has ever happened again. We both learned a lesson that day. We gave and received grace and allowed each other room to mess up.

Proverbs 17:17 reads: *A friend loves at all times . . .* What does it mean to love "at all times"? It means you love your friends, even when they do unlovely things. You give the benefit of the doubt. You work through differences. You realize your friends are human. They make mistakes, and you love them despite their shortcomings.

Giving us room to mess up . . . Boy, Jesus was the best at that! He also taught it in the Sermon on the Mount when he said, "If anyone slaps you on the right cheek, turn to them the other cheek also." (Matthew 5:39) He knew some of his disciples had betrayed him after his arrest, but Jesus came back to them after his resurrection, bearing total forgiveness and unconditional love. Aren't we glad Jesus is our friend and loves us unconditionally, enough to die for us? What if he got mad when we disappointed him, never to speak to us again? That's not the way it works in God's kingdom, and we are supposed to be imitators of Christ in our personal friendships.

I: (Scarf of Truth)
Insecurity in friendships often starts with you.

Let me clarify. Insecurity in friendship often starts in the mind. One way to eliminate this insecurity is by controlling your imagination. How many times have you worried about a friend being mad at you when it turned out there was absolutely nothing wrong? Do you imagine what your friends would think if they knew what a mess your life was? If you have children, does a remark someone makes about "bratty kids" and lenient parents cause you to wonder if they think you're a terrible parent?

Let me illustrate the point with a simple true-life example. Carrie is standing outside in her front yard. A neighborhood friend drives by, looks her way, doesn't stop, and doesn't even wave. How should Carrie interpret her neighbor's actions?

She has a lot on her mind.

She's in a hurry.

Is she mad at me?

That jerk!

You get the point. There are many ways Carrie could think about her neighbor's behavior. Of course, Carrie doesn't know the real reason, so her various explanations all stem from her imagination—and the scenarios are endless. When we are making something up, why don't we make up something that builds up our friendships? Maybe the behavior of Carrie's friend had more to do with how her day was going, rather than with Carrie and her insecurities.

One woman in our survey said she moved frequently in her childhood, and she did not have time to learn how to be a friend. She went on to say that she learned to put up a shield so she wouldn't get hurt when she had to leave her friends behind yet again. She claims, "If you don't know how to be a friend, you don't know how to have friends, even in adulthood."

Have you reached out to women who tend to keep you at arm's length? It may not be about you. It may be that they are afraid of getting too close to another person.

In this case, I think of Jesus and Zacchaeus. You'll find the passage in Luke 19:1–10:

Jesus entered Jericho and was passing through. A man was there by the name of Zacchaeus; he was a chief tax collector and was wealthy. He wanted to see who Jesus was, but because he was short he could not see over the crowd. So he ran ahead and climbed a sycamore-fig tree to see him, since Jesus was coming that way.

When Jesus reached the spot, he looked up and said to him, "Zacchaeus, come down immediately. I must stay at your house today." So he came down at once and welcomed Him gladly.

All the people saw this and began to mutter, "He has gone to be the guest of a sinner."

But Zacchaeus stood up and said to the Lord, "Look, Lord! Here and now I give half of my possessions to the poor, and if I have cheated anybody out of anything, I will pay back four times the amount."

Jesus said to him, "Today salvation has come to this house, because this man, too, is a son of Abraham. For the Son of Man came to seek and to save the lost."

My guess is that when Zacchaeus climbed the tree to get a better look at Jesus, he never dreamed Jesus would come right up to him and speak to him. But once Jesus reached out to him, look what happened. He invited himself to Zacchaeus's house, and Zacchaeus turned his life around! Wow, Jesus was now HIS friend!

Do you know someone who is standoffish? Her distant demeanor may in no way mean that she dislikes you. Maybe she's just shy or new, and you need to invite her down from the tree. Your invitation could be life-changing for that person, as it was with Zacchaeus. When you spot a new woman at church or in a social setting, do you go out of your way to greet her and make her feel welcome? Or maybe you are the one who's climbed up the tree, afraid to get too close to anyone. I advise you to pray someone rescues you from the sycamore. Friendship is worth coming down for.

E: (Scarf of Truth)
Encouraging friends and being honest draw friends closer.

Our friends should be our greatest encouragers. Arnold Glasow, a humorist, once said, "A true friend never gets in your way unless you happen to be going down."[1] In 1 Thessalonians 5:11 God gives us his instructions: "Therefore encourage one another and build each other up, just as in fact you are doing."

In our informal friendship poll, one woman said "a true friendship doesn't feel like a competition, trying to 'one up' each other." Of course, we all love to have friends who don't compete with us and celebrate our success, but it's much harder to be this type of friend. Sometimes when a part of our life doesn't seem to be going well, it's hard to be thrilled about the success of those around us. For example, when Melinda was having trouble with her son's angry outbursts, it was difficult to hear about another friend being told by a teacher she should write a book about parenting because of her exceptional children.

Being an encourager involves a dedication to being aware of how your friend is really doing and offering a hand up when need. As it says in Ecclesiastes 4:9–10, "Two are better than one, because they have a good return for their labor: If either of them falls down, one can help the other up." Are you a cheerleader for your friends? If so, your friend will perceive your support as love, and you'll enjoy a lasting friendship for many years.

Another woman wrote in our poll, "A true friend treats us like we are diamonds, not just cubic zirconia." Remember, most diamonds are beautiful yet flawed. We love them, anyway, don't we, ladies? That's the way we should feel about our friends. We are all flawed, but a good friend still loves us even though we are not perfect!

Jesus was an amazing encourager. When Jesus walked on the water and the disciples were terrified, he immediately said to them,

"Take courage! It is I. Don't be afraid." (Matthew 14:27) Then Peter asked Jesus to tell him to come out to him on the water.

Jesus said, "Come on!" (Lisa Burkhardt Worley translation of Matthew 14:29)

Do we encourage our friends when they are in the midst of what we'd call an impossible task or situation? "Come on! You can do it! I believe in you!" What did Jesus say to the disciples in John 16:33 on the night before he was betrayed? "I have told you these things, so that in me you may have peace. In this world you will have trouble. But take heart! I have overcome the world."

Jesus is saying, don't worry; in the end, everything will be okay. Do we encourage our friends in this way?

Honesty is also an important quality in friendship. If you start hiding your true feelings and thoughts, bricks of deception will form a wall between the two of you. In our informal poll, honesty seemed to be the friendship quality most mentioned. One woman said her friends are good mirrors. Another said she can count on her friends for sound advice. Yet a third added that a true friend can be brutally honest with finesse. Proverbs 27:17 discusses this honesty: "As iron sharpens iron, so one person sharpens another."

Jesus was brutally honest with the twelve who made up his small group. Remember when he spoke to the disciples about his impending death and resurrection in Matthew 16:21–23:

From that time on Jesus began to explain to his disciples that he must go to Jerusalem and suffer many things at the hands of the elders, chief priests and teachers of the law, and that he must be killed and on the third day be raised to life.

Peter took him aside and began to rebuke him. "Never, Lord!" he said. "This shall never happen to you!"

Jesus turned and said to Peter, "Get behind me, Satan! You are a stumbling block to me; you do not have in mind the things of God, but merely human concerns."

Unable to see the big picture, Peter unintentionally tried to thwart God's plan. I don't know about you, but if my friend said to me, "Get behind me, Satan," I might take offense. But you know Jesus loved Peter. Didn't he later describe Peter as the founder of the church, against which the gates of hell would not prevail? This was a case of one friend being extremely honest with another.

N: (Scarf of Truth)
Never be too busy for your friends.

This doesn't mean any time your friends want you to go shopping, you must be available. But it does mean that when a friend is in need, you make a hefty effort to be there.

Matthew 10:39 says: "Whoever finds their life will lose it, and whoever loses their life for my sake will find it." We need to realize our friends' needs are as important to them as our personal needs are to us.

Of course our lives our hectic. Some of us are working and trying to raise a family at the same time. Some of us pour a lot of our time into volunteer work and run, run, run around the clock. But there are things we can give up to be there for our friends. Frankly, some of us need to give up our countless acquaintances so we can be true friends to a few. As Aristotle said, "A friend to all is a friend to none." Some people collect friends. I was asked to be someone's Facebook friend recently, and their account listed over 600 friends! Are all of those people really their friends, I wondered?

Burned out from trying to help too many friends, Grace learned this lesson the hard way. "I wanted everyone to love me, and I desired to love them like Jesus did, so I didn't turn friendships down," she said. "It was emotionally draining to carry everyone's burdens. I became exhausted and had to seek help from a counselor."

The counselor informed her that with her long list of friends, she could not be a great friend to anyone. Her suggestion was to ask God to show her which friends should be "A—top-priority friends," which ones were "B—see-occasionally friends," and, finally, the "C friends." She advised Grace to concentrate on her top-priority friends and to quit stretching herself so thin trying to do for everyone. Grace also learned that if she didn't stop taking care of everyone but herself, eventually she might not be able to be there for anyone, not even her "A" friends. Good advice for Grace, and good advice for us.

In our poll, a woman said she has few, but very close friends. She finds that when she becomes friends with someone who has many superficial friendships, expectations of the friendship often clash. Are you one who has a lot of friends, but none of them are terribly close? Another woman wrote that her close friends are people she can call with an emergency, and they will drop everything to listen, talk, and help. She, in return, would do or has done the same for them. She defined an "emergency friend" as "someone who cares about me." In other words, if you are having an emotional emergency day, that friend is the one on the other end of the 911 call.

Are you an "emergency" friend? Are your friends "emergency" friends to you, and do they deeply care about you? When a friend texts you with a pressing situation or prayer need, do you get right back to her if you can?

When a friend's daughter was injured in a soccer accident, my friend reached out to me. I immediately texted people to start a prayer chain, then raced to the hospital, forty-five minutes away, where her daughter was undergoing emergency surgery. I knew my friend needed me, and I wanted to be with her, give her a hug, and show my love and support.

That day, I was an emergency friend to her. Are you never too busy for friends, or do you say, "I'll get to them later?" Proverbs 18:24 is right on: "One who has unreliable friends soon comes to ruin, but there is a friend who sticks closer than a brother." I don't know about you, but I don't have any brothers or sisters in my life, and when I make a female friend, I want them to be like a sister to me. That's what I need and desire in a friendship. Making friends a priority makes friends feel loved.

D: (Scarf of Truth)
Divine bonds are powerful in friendships.

There is something mighty special about a friend who shares your faith. King David had a great friend of fellowship in Jonathan. First Samuel 18:1 says: "After David had finished talking with Saul, Jonathan became one in spirit with David, and he loved him as himself." Even when Jonathan's dad, King Saul, became insanely jealous of David, Jonathan helped his friend escape when he realized his father wanted to kill David. Through his faith in God, he knew saving his friend was the right thing to do, even if it meant going against his father. When David and Jonathan knew they would no longer be able to hang out together, this was their exchange: "Then they kissed each other and wept together—but David wept the most. Jonathan said to David, 'Go in peace, for we have sworn friendship with each other in the name of the LORD, saying, The LORD is witness between you and me, and between your descendants and my descendants forever.'"(1 Samuel 20:41–42)

What was their promise? They promised always to be loyal friends to each other.

In our informal poll, a woman who participates in a Christian accountability group says her accountability sisters are her closest friends. They meet once a week and keep their conversation focused on Christ. Serving others together and laughing together strengthens their friendship bond. Another woman explains that her long-term friendships share a common set of beliefs that point to Christ's presence in our lives today; they encourage each other to become stronger in their Christian walks through prayer, study, and service to others. She goes on to explain that these friendships are evidence of "God's love with skin on," and direct her to the best path in decision making. One of my closest long-term friends is someone I met in a small group Bible study.

Can you relate to these kinds of divine bonds with friends? What about our divine bond with Jesus? Many times, Jesus refers to believers as friends, and the key to being a friend of Jesus is laid out in John 15:12–17:

> "My command is this: Love each other as I have loved you. Greater love has no one than this: to lay down one's life for one's friends. You are my friends if you do what I command. I no longer call you servants, because a servant does not know his master's business. Instead, I have called you friends, for everything that I learned from my Father I have made known to you. You did not choose me, but I chose you and appointed you so that you might go and bear fruit—fruit that will last—and so that whatever you ask in my name the Father will give you. This is my command: Love each other."

So how do we become a friend of Jesus? The answer is three words: "love one another." We need to love all those God brings into our path and ask to see them through his eyes. We should also ask his help to love those who are not so loveable. Then we are a true friend of Jesus, who lavishes us with unconditional love. He loves us like no other. No matter who cuts us out of their life, Jesus will never sever his divine bond with us. He is the diamond-quality friend without flaws. He is our emergency friend, on call 24–7. He is the one who calls us down from the tree to have a relationship with him. He is the friend who gave his life for us, and all he asks from us is to follow him and let his love flow through us to others.

So who would you add to the list of famous friend duos we began with? Lucy and Ethel; Thelma and Louise; Wilma and Betty; Astro and George Jetson; how about adding another dynamic duo to that list that can't be outdone, outlasted, or beat: Jesus and you. Now, that has a nice ring to it!

Gloves of Prayer: *Gracious Lord, guide me in my quest for friends. Bring to me those you want in my life. Help me to be slow to anger and quick to love. Slow to judge and quick to forgive. Remind me that no one, including me, is perfect. Show me how to be transparent with my friends and honest, without a hidden agenda. Lord, remove a spirit of jealousy from me. Enable me to be my friends' cheerleader and always want the best for them. In Jesus' name, AMEN.*

Discussion Questions:
If I Only Had . . . Closer Friendships

1. Do you believe "If I Only Had . . . Closer Friendships" you'd be more secure?

2. Friendships are important because God designed us to connect with each other. Which famous friendships are most appealing to you from the Bible or television? David and Jonathan? Mary and Elizabeth? Thelma and Louise? Wilma and Betty? Astro and George? Why?

3. Describe an important friendship in your life. What makes this friendship special? What drew you to this person, or how did you meet? What makes you close? Why do you think you are still friends?

4. Describe a friendship that causes you to feel insecure. As you read this chapter, did God give you insight into the reason for your insecurity? Do you pray God will heal your insecurity?

5. Friendships should be about whom God wants in our lives. Have you ever been aware of God supplying you with a specific friendship? Do you ask God to bring people into your life who will help you grow in godliness?

6. Just as Martha was hurt by her running buddies no longer including her, think of a time you were hurt by a friend. Did God bring any good out of the situation? If not and if it's still painful, how can you allow God to still work good out of this pain?

7. The Scripture 1 Thessalonians 5:11 instructs us to encourage one another and build each other up. How do you encourage your friends?

8. There are many stories of friendships in this chapter: Which story resonates with you most: Martha and her running buddies, Becky and the big-hair Texas woman, Lisa and the friend who didn't wait, or Grace and the long list of friends?

9. The scarves of truth in this chapter spell out the acrostic FRIENDS. Which scarf of truth have you recently seen demonstrated in your life: forcing friendships doesn't work; give your friends room to mess up; insecurity starts with you; encourage friends and be honest; never be too busy for a friend; divine bonds are powerful?

10. There is something mighty special about a friend who shares your faith. In your opinion, what makes godly friends so special? List your godly friends and ways in which they have brought you closer to Christ.

Ten

If I Only Had . . .
More Money

AS I CAME HOME from elementary school one day, an official-looking envelope bearing my name lay on the counter. My paternal grandmother had recently died, and this registered letter held information about her last will and testament. I hesitated to open it. You see, my dad's mother hadn't been in my life. After I was born in San Antonio, Texas, this grandmother and an aunt came to visit me. Upon seeing my mother's depressed mental state due to the death of my father two months before my birth, my grandmother demanded to take me back to Chicago to raise me.

My maternal grandmother told me there was a standoff concerning this plan, which she won, saying, "You'll take this baby over my dead body!" My paternal grandmother was a wealthy woman, so despite her unfriendly encounter with my maternal grandmother, I hoped she might have some compassion for my situation growing up, as my mother and I lived near poverty. Opening the letter and then unfolding it, I scanned it for an amount.

There toward the bottom in bold numbers, the amount $1.00 stared back at me. Even as young as I was, I was shocked and hurt by this because I knew what it meant. My grandmother had disinherited me, while other children and grandchildren split a sizeable amount between them.

I learned early in life that my inheritance was not on this earth. For me, the money did not represent financial stability; it represented my grandmother's love for me. Even at eight years old, I felt abandoned by my grandmother due to her action. Her last will and testament was an exclamation point enforcing her rejection. For me, money was—and still is—a heart issue.

Scarf of Truth:
God uses money as a barometer of our heart condition.

With over two thousand references to money in the Bible, God knows what a huge stumbling block money can be for us, and he also knows that how we spend money reveals our priorities. Have you ever gone through your checkbook to see where your money goes? It usually indicates what's important to you. Is most of your extra cash earmarked for clothes or pampering, or does much of it go to the church or toward helping others in need? In both Matthew and Luke, it states, "For where your treasure is, there your heart will be also." (Matthew 6:21)

Remember the story of the rich young ruler who desired to follow Christ? In *The Message* version of Mark 10:17–22, he asked Jesus, whom he referred to as the "good teacher," what he needed to do to inherit eternal life:

> Jesus said, "Why are you calling me good? No one is good, only God. You know the commandments: Don't murder, don't commit adultery, don't steal, don't lie, don't cheat, honor your father and mother."
>
> He said, "Teacher, I have—from my youth—kept them all!"
>
> Jesus looked him hard in the eye—and loved him! He said, "There's one thing left: Go sell whatever you own and give it to the

poor. All your wealth will then be heavenly wealth. And come follow me."

The man's face clouded over. This was the last thing he expected to hear, and he walked off with a heavy heart. He was holding on tight to a lot of things, and not about to let go.

The rich young ruler followed all the commandments, but Jesus asked him to take the next step. Jesus was getting a reading on his heart by requesting such a drastic measure. I can almost hear the rich man groan. Jesus, for his part, already knew that for this young ruler, having wealth was more important than having a relationship with him. Material things were in first place, not Jesus.

Jesus may not ask us to give up our earthly wealth, but he may ask us to restructure what we do with it. Look at your checkbook and credit card statements, calculate how much of your money is spent on things of God, and how much of your money is spent on things of pleasure. This will determine where your heart lies.

King Solomon had a healthy understanding that money and the heart are connected, and realized early on that money can compete with our spiritual journey. The book of Proverbs, attributed to Solomon, is loaded with wisdom teachings about this very concept. Here are a few of Solomon's greatest hits. Proverbs 1:19: "Such are the paths of all who go after ill-gotten gain; it takes away the life of those who get it." Proverbs 11:28: "Those who trust in their riches will fall, but the righteous will thrive like a green leaf." Proverbs 16:8: "Better a little with righteousness than much gain with injustice."

Has the desire for money robbed you of life? Do you feel like your problems might be solved by money? Do you believe your life would improve if you only had . . . money?

Solomon would have made the Forbes wealthiest list but he still had his issues. In 2 Chronicles 9:13, it states: "The weight of the gold that Solomon received yearly was 666 talents . . ." That did not include the money brought to him by merchants and traders, as well as by the kings and governors of the land. One talent was worth about $14,000, so Solomon brought in a cool nine million-plus per year!

In 2 Chronicles 9:22 it speaks to Solomon's affluence: "King Solomon was greater in riches and wisdom than all the other kings of the earth." However, toward the end of his life, Solomon reflected in Ecclesiastes 2:10–11: "I denied myself nothing my eyes desired; I refused my heart no pleasure. My heart took delight in all my labor, and this was the reward for all my toil. Yet when I surveyed all that my hands had done and what I had toiled to achieve, everything was meaningless, a chasing after the wind; nothing was gained under the sun."

After a lifetime of incredible wealth, Solomon discovered that money does not buy happiness.

Howard Hughes was a billionaire who seemed to have it all. Successful businessman, movie producer, and an aviator, he spent his later years in seclusion. Hughes became such a hermit that when he died in 1976 aboard an airplane, the Treasury Department had to use fingerprints to confirm his death. In Hughes's case, it is apparent Solomon was right; everything was meaningless.

We know of many other celebrities who appeared fulfilled through fame and money, but they ended up anesthetizing themselves with drugs. In the past twenty years, comedians John Belushi and Chris Farley, actors River Phoenix and Heath Ledger were rich, successful stars who died due to drug overdoses. Apparently, money did not buy them happiness either. Do you think you will be happier if you have more money?

Scientists from Boston and British Columbia decided to find out whether money really can buy happiness. They were troubled by the fact that over the past twenty to thirty years, people in the U.S., as well as other developed countries, made a lot more money than less-developed countries, but happiness was less evident. Interestingly enough, they discovered that money could buy happiness—but only when spent on someone else. In one experiment, the scientists asked volunteers to rate their happiness. They gave each subject some cash, either five or twenty dollars. Half the participants were told to spend the money on themselves. The others were asked to give it away. At the end of the day, the people who received the biggest boost were the ones who shared the wealth, even if it was only five dollars.

Scarf of Truth:
God often uses money problems to redirect our lives.

After I rededicated my life to Christ, I prayed six years for my husband to make Christ his Lord, as well. In the midst of my prayers, my husband's new golf business began to struggle, and his paychecks stopped. I did my best to plug up all the holes of our sinking ship with my paycheck, but I couldn't keep the flood of household bills under control. Bill collectors called every day, and eventually, after months of missed mortgage payments, the bank threatened to put our house on the auction block. Just when I thought I couldn't take it anymore, God reminded me of my prayer for my husband, and it became clear—the Lord was using this financial crisis to get my husband's attention and redirect him.

When he had reached an all-time low, my husband responded to the pressure by going on a spiritual retreat, where he rededicated his life to Christ. Following the retreat, my husband gave up his entrepreneurial business—difficult for him to do—and went to work for another company so he could start catching up on the household bills. In the midst of his transformation, the Holy Spirit also convicted him to tithe. When God asked us to tithe, we still had not recovered from our financial crisis. It was not the best time to begin the tithing discipline, as it never is, but God blessed our obedience.

What happened over the following years was a miracle. God restored our finances so we no longer struggled with money issues.

In addition, we began to grow spiritually as a couple, hosting group Bible studies in our home. My husband also became a small group facilitator for Crown Financial Ministry.

Malachi 3:10 challenges us, "Bring the whole tithe into the storehouse, that there may be food in my house. Test me in this," says the LORD Almighty, "and see if I will not throw open the floodgates of heaven and pour out so much blessing that there will not be room enough to store it."

Malachi 3:10 is the only place in the Bible where God allows us to test him, and the testing concerns money.

New Testament Christians not only tithed but gave offerings above the tithe for church maintenance, as well as alms for the poor. Currently, the average Christian gives just over two percent of his or her income to the Lord. Do you love money more than God? Do you believe everything belongs to God? He lets us keep ninety percent and asks for just ten percent back. In our case, Malachi 3:10 rang true. God opened the floodgates of heaven and provided for all our needs. In addition, God became the center of our marriage, and we revolved around him, not money.

Scarf of Truth:
Money is not the answer to our problems. God is.

Later, the Lord once again used money to stretch our faith when I received the call to seminary. As I lay on the beach one day, God told me I needed to quit my full-time job so I could focus on seminary—definitely not a thought I would concoct! God knew seminary would take energy and time, and I couldn't be a mom, work full-time, go to school part-time, and do any of it well. At the time, the idea seemed absurd, and I boldly told God in so many words it was too far-fetched to consider. Our current financial arrangement was all my husband knew. We needed my salary so the checking account balance would register black, and not bright-red. So, I made a deal with God—a practice that is not advised. I told him if he wanted me to quit my job, he would need to replace my salary in my husband's income, and it would have to be my husband's idea for me to quit.

Nothing happened initially. I continued to toil away at my full-time job the first year of school, and found that working, taking care of two boys, and attending class took its toll on me. Twice, during mid-terms and finals, I suffered panic attacks while studying for my exams. The emergency room doctor told me he saw it all the time in working students. Their brains are fried because of the added stress of school, so the body reacts negatively. I was given some anti-anxiety medication and told to take it easy.

However, during that year, we also began to see God at work. First, my husband's pay increased—so much so, that it almost replaced my salary. God was holding up his end of the deal. Then, one day, after watching how my schedule drained my strength, my husband suggested I quit work to concentrate on the kids and seminary. There was still a piece of my salary that had not been recovered, but my husband saw it as a leap of faith.

I realized that as I had asked God, it was my husband's idea for me to quit working. I turned in my resignation, and not long after, the remaining chunk of my salary was replaced in my husband's pay. It was amazing what happened in our lives as soon as we gave God access to the money he provided us!

Scarf of Truth:
God wants us to give others access to our excess.

In the early days of the church, shortly after Jesus' resurrection, believers shared with each other and helped out those in need.

All the believers were one in heart and mind. No one claimed that any of their possessions was their own, but they shared everything they had. With great power the apostles continued to testify to the resurrection of the Lord Jesus. And God's grace was so powerfully at work in them all that there were no needy persons among them. For from time to time those who owned land or houses sold them, brought the money from the sales and put it at the apostles' feet, and it was distributed to anyone who had need. (Acts 4:32–35)

Does this seem impossible for us today? It can happen! Here's a current day example of an Acts 4 mentality: My brother-in-law and sister-in-law were involved in a near-plane crash about nine years ago. Sue and her husband, Jim, were on a Comair flight headed from the Bahamas to Orlando when the plane, because of ice build-up on the wings, did a barrel roll and plummeted 8,000 feet in about twenty-four seconds.

When this all happened, my sister-in-law prayed over and over, *Lord, please save us! Lord, please save us!*

Then she clearly heard a voice say, *It's not your time yet, Sue.*

After she received that message from God, the plane leveled out from its noisy descent into the Atlantic Ocean and made an emergency landing in West Palm Beach.

It wasn't my sister-in-law's time yet. To show their gratitude to God for saving their lives, my sister-in-law and brother-in-law gave all the proceeds from the sale of their rental house to the church, about $70,000. In a sense, they were laying the proceeds of this house at the apostles' feet. Specifically, they laid the money—everything they received from the sale of the house—at the door of their church. They gave their church access to their excess.

How can we emerge from our obsession with money and transform it to an obsession with helping the poor? Is there a way for people to have access to your excess? How is Christian living supposed to look today?

I know one woman who started a food pantry for families in the church who were in need. Troubled by the need she saw, she and her family downsized their house so they would have more excess to help others. While some of us may be wearing the latest fashions, there are so many who don't even have the basics, whether it's enough food, or money to pay bills around the house. What can we deny ourselves so we can send a gift card to someone to use at the local grocery store? When we give God access to our excess, he will move us to keep on giving.

A Gallup poll conducted in 2011 stated the majority of Americans believe they need to make an annual income of $150,000 in order to be rich.[1] The average income for the U.S. is around $41,000. When you take a gander at the rest of the world, you can see why this thinking is so distorted. According to Nations Online, the average annual income in Thailand is $3,760, compared to about $13,000 in Argentina. The average income of a citizen in Malawi is $596 yearly.[2] For many of us, Malawi's annual income would amount to two weeks of groceries for our household! I wonder how many times someone in Malawi has pondered, "If I only had . . . more money." Part of giving God access to your excess is letting God open your eyes to how much excess you really have.

Time and time again, the Bible encourages us to have a heart for the poor, and to be like the Acts 4 church, sharing everything we have. If you are not helping others, where do you begin? Where is your excess?

You have excess clothes, so make a deal with yourself that you cannot go shopping for anything new until you give things away. How many items in your closet sit idle on the hanger, gathering dust, crying out to be worn by someone who has no wardrobe?

Do you have excess change making your wallet fat? Empty your loose change into a jar, choose a cause or person, and when it's full, donate it.

If you eat out in excess, cut back, and share that money with others who can't put food on the table.

Do you have excess furniture in your house, just taking up

space in your attic? Find a non-profit charity who would love to take the pieces of furniture off your hands!

There are so many opportunities to allow those in need to have access to our excess.

In his writings to both Jewish and Gentile believers, James comes down hard on the wealthy in *The Message* version of James 5:2–3 he says: "Your greedy luxuries are a cancer in your gut, destroying your life from within. You thought you were piling up wealth. What you've piled up is judgment." According to the *HarperCollins Bible Commentary*, James is not condemning wealth but is condemning the greed and injustice involved in creating it.[3] In James 5:5-6, the terminology is stronger: "You have lived on earth in luxury and self-indulgence. You have fattened yourselves in the day of slaughter. You have condemned and murdered the innocent one, who was not opposing you."

You think, *James, that's a bit harsh! Just because I have a few luxuries doesn't mean I'm destroying life.* But in a sense, it does. We live in excess despite the fact that 2,500 children die every day in Africa because there is not enough clean water. Due to food shortages in Africa, as many as 14,000,000 people are at a risk of starvation or malnutrition. Closer to home, according to a September 11, 2011, New York Times article, 46.2 million people exist below the official poverty line, the highest number since the Census Bureau started tracking this statistic fifty-six years ago.[4] A few dollars from our excess could go a long way toward saving a life in Africa or providing a meal for someone here in the United States.

When we give, we are giving as Christ calls us to give and caring as Christ calls us to care in Matthew 25:34–40:

> "Then the King will say to those on his right, 'Come, you who are blessed by my Father; take your inheritance, the kingdom prepared for you since the creation of the world. For I was hungry and you gave me something to eat, I was thirsty and you gave me something

to drink, I was a stranger and you invited me in, I needed clothes and you clothed me, I was sick and you looked after me, I was in prison and you came to visit me.'

"Then the righteous will answer him, 'Lord, when did we see you hungry and feed you, or thirsty and give you something to drink? When did we see you a stranger and invite you in, or needing clothes and clothe you? When did we see you sick or in prison and go to visit you?'

"The King will reply, 'Truly I tell you, whatever you did for one of the least of these brothers and sisters of mine, you did for me.'"

Do we focus on what we don't have financially, or do we figure out ways to help others with the resources we do have?

Scarf of Truth:
Money should never influence how we treat others.

Elizabeth saw how increased wealth changed the people she lived around. She grew up lower-middle-class in a Texas oil town. Her father was a government worker, not involved in the oil business, but she would watch the dynamics of her community change during the various oil booms. "When an oil boom would hit," Elizabeth remembered, "the people across the street from me would move across town and have pools. I saw what money can do to people. I would be welcome at their tables one year, and not the next. It made me wonder what was so important about money; why rich people congregate together and why poor people have this outside looking-in distrust of them."

Now a middle-aged adult, Elizabeth has a heart for those who struggle with money issues. To help others, she spends some of her free time serving as a small-group leader in the Dave Ramsey Financial Peace Ministry. She still sees how money affects families negatively, with many of the people in her small groups carrying debt from fifty to two hundred thousand dollars. "People are obsessed with the things that have a great financial impact on their life. They can be obsessed about the house they live in, their neighborhood, the iPhone 3, 4 or 5. Does it boil down to, *I am afraid people won't accept me for who I am if I don't have the right purse, golf club, boat, or shoes?* One woman in my small group wondered if she should give up her weekly manicures so she could save for her child's college. I think money is the biggest temptation that separates you from God."

Do material things separate you from God? Do you treat others differently if they have money? Jesus never discriminated against anyone because of social status. Among his closest friends and followers there were a variety of people representing different economic levels, including fishermen, a doctor, a not-so-popular tax collector, and a woman who had been demon-possessed. What an interesting assortment of people, but he loved them all the same. That's the example he sets. We should love everyone unconditionally, whether rich or poor, important in the world's eyes or not.

Scarf of Truth:
Money should be used for eternal purposes.

One of my friends recently told me about how her nephew has changed the way he gives money. He is a recovering drug addict, and a fairly new Christian who commented, "I used to give all my money to the devil and his boys; now I give it to God."

When it comes to money, we need to think with a focus on eternity, not on this world. Matthew 6:19–21 exhorts us: "Do not store up for yourselves treasures on earth, where moths and vermin destroy and where thieves break in and steal. But store up for yourselves treasures in heaven, where moths and vermin do not destroy, and where thieves do not break in and steal. For where your treasure is, there your heart will be also."

Did you know that in 2008, the mini-storage industry in the United States had total sales in excess of twenty-billion dollars? There are 58,000 mini storage facilities worldwide. 52,000 of them are in the United States.[5] The average American house size has more than doubled since the 1950s, while the average household size has decreased, but we still don't have enough room in our houses to store all our stuff. What are we using our money for?

Nationally known author and pastor, Rick Warren, reverse-tithes. He gives away 90 percent of his income to those in need and keeps 10 percent.[6] Through the Bill and Melinda Gates Foundation, the Gateses are giving away $60 billion.[7] Their priorities are health and education in developing countries. What about you? Most of us don't have sixty billion to give away, but how are you storing up treasures in heaven? One small way I store up treasures in heaven is by giving away Christian books. If I believe a particular book might help someone else, I'll buy it for them. It's not a huge expense, but it is a means of furthering the kingdom. When I was in seminary, I offered a ride to another seminary student and never asked for gas money because I knew she struggled financially. It was my way of helping her out during tough times. A friend of mine conducts a homeless drive every Christmas, gathering coats, hats, and gloves for a group of people who make their permanent residence under a bridge. You won't have to look far to find practical ways to store up treasures in heaven.

When we focus on eternity, we should pray before making any large spending decisions, and ask God where he wants us to give. I needed a rug in my dining room, so a friend told me about a sale on rugs at a local department store. My husband gave me a budget that he asked me to stay within. When we arrived at the store, the area rug I liked was over my budget, so I prayed that if I was supposed to buy that particular rug, the store would come down on the price. When I asked the sales person whether he could do better on the price, he did lower the amount on the ticket, making it affordable. My friend claimed she had never seen anyone pray about a buying decision like that. It was a witness to her!

When we ask God to show us where he wants us to give, he will often bring a need to the forefront, giving us an opportunity to give them access to our excess. My husband and I have used our excess to send anonymous gift cards to those who might be in a difficult season of their life financially, simply because God brought them to our attention and called us to help.

God blesses us financially to bless others. A friend of mine who is a nail technician told me the story of how God answered her prayer to send her daughter to a private Christian school. She shared that dream with one of her clients, who then offered to pay for four years of Christian education for her daughter. My friend turned the offer down at first because she didn't want her wealthy client to think she was baiting her to do it; she was just sharing her dream with her. But then she thought, *Maybe this is the way God is answering my prayer. If she asks again, I will accept her offer.*

The next time she saw her client, the offer was presented again. The client said when she gives away money to help someone, God is always faithful to return it to her tenfold. So, my friend's dream of sending her daughter to a Christian school became reality, because a woman gave her daughter access to her excess.

Being used by Christ in a significant way has nothing to do with a high position or great riches. It has everything to do with a willingness to allow Christ to become your Lord. This also means allowing him to be Lord over your wealth. Imagine yourself at the pearly gates with God before you, surrounded by the other saints. When you are asked by God to give an account of your finances over your lifetime, will you be embarrassed, or will you be redeeming all the treasures you built up in heaven? It's not too late to make some changes. God will bless your obedience with a heavenly inheritance only he can provide.

Gloves of Prayer: *Lord God, I know money is not the answer to my problems. You are the only answer, Lord, because the happiness money buys is fleeting. Teach me how to be wiser in the way I handle money so I can build up an inheritance in heaven, rather than on earth. Convict me to bring the whole tithe to your storehouse as an act of love toward you. In Jesus' name, AMEN.*

Discussion Questions:
If I Only Had . . . More Money

1. Lisa's grandmother disinherited her while other children and grandchildren split a sizeable amount between them. She learned early in life that her inheritance was not on this earth. Do you believe. "If I only had . . . more money" you'd be more secure?

2. With over two thousand references to money in the Bible, God knows what a huge stumbling block money can be for us. He also knows that how we spend money demonstrates our priorities. How has money been a stumbling block for you in your relationships with people and God?

3. Jesus may not ask us to give up our earthly wealth, but he may ask us to restructure what we do with the money we have. Take some time to look at your credit card statements, and see how your money is spent. Is God calling you to restructure what you do with your money? What would that look like in your life?

4. Solomon would have made the Forbes wealthiest list but he still had his issues. In 2 Chronicles 9:13, it states: "The weight of the gold that Solomon received yearly was 666 talents." How can the appearance of wealth be a facade for happiness? Do you think King Solomon was happy? Can you think of others, in more current times, who seem to have it all but cannot find happiness?

5. Lisa prayed six years for her husband to make Christ his Lord. In the midst of her prayers, her husband's new golf business began to struggle, and his paychecks stopped. Has God ever

used money problems to redirect your life? If so, how?

6. God told Lisa to quit her full-time job so she could focus on seminary. It seemed absurd at first because they needed both pay checks to balance the books, but as God continued to increase her husband's salary she took the step of obedience. Has God ever taken care of you financially when having enough money seemed impossible?

7. God wants us to give others access to our excess. Matthew 25: 34–36 says, "Then the King will say to those on his right, 'Come, you who are blessed by my Father; take your inheritance the kingdom prepared for you since the creation of the world. For I was hungry and you gave me something to eat, I was thirsty and you gave me something to drink, I was a stranger and you invited me in, I needed clothes and you clothed me, I was sick and you looked after me, I was in prison and you came to visit me.'" How can you bless others with your bounty?

8. Elizabeth saw how increased wealth changed the people she lived around. She grew up lower-middle-class in a Texas oil town. Her father was a government worker, not involved in the oil business, but she watched the dynamics of her community change during oil booms. Be honest. Has someone's social standing ever affected how you acted around them? If so, why do you think that person's affluence affected you?

9. Matthew 6:19–21 tells us to avoid storing up treasures on earth. Consider for a minute and then list the spiritual dangers of having more money. How can material possessions

separate you from God?

10. Money should be used for eternal purposes. Have you ever prayed before making a spending decision? What steps can you take to improve the way you make decisions about money?

Eleven

If I Only Had . . .
Beauty

THE YEAR I TURNED seventeen, Janis Ian recorded a hit song called, "At Seventeen." At the time, I thought this song was written just for me because it seemed to capture the essence of my life. For those of you who don't remember the lyrics, it's written from the point of view of a forlorn, unattractive girl who longs for romance. She sits alone on Friday nights realizing love was only meant for "beauty queens."

Can you relate? I wore glasses most of my high school years, and I lived "Boys don't make passes at girls who wear glasses." I played basketball during high school and like clockwork, one of the thick lenses from my glasses popped out at every game. I was gawky not only at seventeen but also as a pre-teen.

During my senior year of high school, I began wearing contact lenses. In the spring semester of that year, I went to visit the college I ultimately attended. During lunch, I was serving myself at the salad bar when a nice-looking, tall football player came up to ask if I planned to attend the party later that night. Looking around, my friend spoke up and said, "Lisa, he's speaking to you."

I had never dreamed anyone would find me attractive enough

to wonder if I was going to a party.

Do you ever wonder whether you are beautiful enough? Frankly, in our society it's difficult to be secure about our looks. We are bombarded by ads and messages that constantly point out where we fall short.

We often see ourselves and others inaccurately because we don't have God's corrected vision. Do you remember standing in front of a funhouse mirror and laughing at your short legs, wide hips, and watermelon-sized head? While this example may be drastic, we often view ourselves in a similar, inaccurate way. Let's look at a few of these mirrors and lenses that warp our view of what beauty truly entails.

Scarf of Truth:
When it comes to beauty, we often look at ourselves under a magnifying glass.

Have you ever stood in front of a mirror staring at a blemish? As you gawk, it seems to grow on your face until you see nothing but a giant red mountain. The same is true for our beauty. The more we concentrate on the extra pounds on our hips, or our nose that's too big, or the wrinkles that line our face, the worse these minor imperfections seem.

How many times have you asked yourself, "Does anyone think I'm pretty?" Maybe you're still stuck in a low self-image that developed when you were a teenager. I still have this problem. I remember looking at old photos, and at the time, I thought I looked terrible, but then ten years later, I'd look at them again and think, *Hmm . . . I wasn't that bad.* I remember someone from a Bible study saying to me about herself, "If I'd known how cute I was back then, I would have been trouble!"

We're not alone in how we view ourselves. Our culture is obsessed with beauty, which makes women insecure about the way they appear. According to a YWCA Report, called "Beauty At Any Cost," in the year 2007, there were 11.7 million cosmetic procedures performed in the United States. That's an increase of nearly 500 percent in the overall number of procedures in the ten years prior to 2007.[1]

You may be familiar with Jocelyn Wildenstein. She was a beautiful woman in the 1970s, but in an effort to win her husband back after he committed adultery, she went under the knife and spent about four million dollars on plastic surgery.[2] Trying to perfect her eyes, cheekbones and lips left her face deformed.

I recently saw an interview with a former super model now in her sixties. It was apparent she'd had plastic surgery because when she spoke, her face hardly moved, and it looked like a costume mask. A friend of mine also interviewed an aging country music singer, and said from a distance she looked great, but when she got right up on her, she looked ridiculous because of all the work she's had done. Comedian Joan Rivers jokes about her cosmetic procedures when she admits she can no longer feel her face.

I admire actress Meryl Streep, now sixty years old, for going against the Hollywood grain. In a *Good Housekeeping* magazine article, Streep says she's seen her peers undergo drastic plastic surgery trying to hold on to youth. "It's not just women," she says. "You'd be amazed at how many men in this industry have gone down that road. I just don't get it. You have to embrace getting older. Life is precious, and when you've lost a lot of people, you realize each day is a gift."[3]

Meryl Streep is on to something.

Scarf of Truth:
Our sense of personal beauty can't be defined by society's airbrushed standards.

I can still picture my eighth grade English teacher, Mrs. Collie. I thought she was stunning, but not because she was young and hip. She was older, tall, with smooth, white hair. I think it was the way she carried herself that made her beautiful. She was a good teacher, sophisticated, kind, and she was a lady. That's not how the world judges beauty today, is it?

We have to remember that most of the attractive people we see on magazine covers have been airbrushed. In fact, according to expert photographer and retoucher, Tim Lynch, ninety-nine percent of the celebrity photos you see in the media have been altered. In an interview with Diet.com, Lynch said, "When you talk about the Hollywood types, they have a personal retoucher that does this all day long, and they pay them really well. Not one picture is released without their permission. It's just the way they want to be viewed by the world. They want to have this sort of perfection, which is not possible."[4]

Women aren't the only ones who get touched-up. Tennis star Andy Roddick appeared on the June/July cover of *Men's Fitness Magazine*, and apparently the editors believed Roddick wasn't quite fit enough. They ballooned the size of Roddick's biceps to better entice readers with the headline, "How to Build Big Arms."[5]

In a 2002 issue of *More Magazine*, Jamie Lee Curtis posed for a "before" and "after" picture to demonstrate what happens on a photo shoot. In her "before" photo, she wore spandex shorts and a bra, no makeup, and no manicure. She looks like an average soccer mom with a bit of a tummy, thighs with a little extra meat, and a love handle hanging over her shorts. Then, after a hairstylist, makeup artist, fancy clothes, and a little retouching, she transformed to *vavoom!*[6]

In one case, the Brits decided to take a stand. A July 2011 article on MSNBC's website reported that a number of L'Oreal print advertisements, starring Julia Roberts and Christy Turlington, were banned in Britain after determining the amount of airbrushing used was misleading. The British Advertising Standards Authority found the digitally enhanced ads did not accurately reflect what could be achieved from Maybelline's "The Eraser" and Lancôme's

"Teint Miracle" foundation products. L'Oreal owns both Maybelline and Lancôme. The Lancôme advertisement featuring Julia Roberts was not a before-and-after shot, but a heavily enhanced photograph of her instead. Lancôme claimed the images of Roberts accurately portrayed what a customer could hope to achieve, but due to contractual obligations, they could not provide any non-airbrushed photos of Roberts.[7]

Even Jesus has been airbrushed throughout the years. Many artists make Jesus out to be a hottie. But in reality, the Bible does not say that Jesus had physical beauty. It is quite the opposite. In a prophecy about Jesus in Isaiah 53:2, the description states, "He grew up before him like a tender shoot, and like a root out of dry ground. He had no beauty or majesty to attract us to him, nothing in his appearance that we should desire him."

Nothing in his appearance that we should desire him, but we do desire him, don't we? It's not about his physical beauty. It's about the character of Jesus; it's his heart, not physical beauty, that we long for.

We cannot base our sense of beauty on the world's standards because that beauty is not real. They take an already gorgeous model, spend hours on her hair and makeup, and then when that is done, they edit out any remaining imperfections. It's unattainable beauty, but unfortunately, many women still try to attain it at any cost. Eating disorders, cosmetic surgery, and low self-esteem are all symptoms of the issue of gauging ourselves against these photo-enhanced images.

Scarf of Truth:
We will be more secure if we don't compare ourselves to others.

Comparing ourselves to others is like constantly changing the focus on our camera. When we are with our skinny friend, we focus on her skinniness and feel fat. When we are with our fancy friend, we feel dumpy. When we are with our youthful friends, we feel old. My husband says there will always be someone richer, younger, or better looking than you. So constantly comparing ourselves with others leaves us on ever-shifting sand.

Comparing is also unrealistic. I might want Brittany's hair, Samantha's height, Sally's wrinkle-free skin, and Joyce's figure, but we can't go through a cafeteria line and order up the perfect bodies. If we did, I'm sure we'd be a mess. We are a whole package. When we compare, we never compare the whole package, life and all. I have a friend who always says we should not compare someone else's outsides to our insides. They may have a beautiful face or body, but their insides may be an ugly mess! Some of the most beautiful people I've known over the years have also been some of the unhappiest people I've known. Beauty does not equal happiness. Neither do skinniness or youthful looks.

Psalm 139:15–16 says, "My frame was not hidden from you when I was made in the secret place, when I was woven together in the depths of the earth. Your eyes saw my unformed body; all the days ordained for me were written in your book before one of them came to be." This verse is saying God wove you together just the way he wanted you to be. You are one of his precious pieces of art!

One of the moms at my son's school is so pretty she could stop traffic. That was intimidating to me at first, but as I got to know her, I found out she is a strong Christian, and as beautiful on the inside as she is on the outside. I enjoy talking to her, and that wall of insecurity I'd built up between the two of us began to crumble as I looked past her appearance.

Have you ever avoided someone because their outward appearance intimidated you? We must remember that being insecure around beautiful people prohibits God from using us in their lives. Our joy should come from sharing our faith with all people. Are you letting your insecurities prevent you from sharing Christ with the physically beautiful?

Magnifying glasses, airbrushed lenses, and our ever-changing comparison focus: these ways of evaluating ourselves and others breed insecurity. There is only one way to find security with our looks, and that is by using God's looking glass.

Scarf of Truth:
To understand what real beauty is, we must consult the Bible.

The Bible, after all, is God's love letter to his people. In 1 Peter 3:3–4 the Word gives us a clue of what godly beauty looks like: "Your beauty should not come from outward adornment, such as elaborate hairstyles and the wearing of gold jewelry or fine clothes. Rather, it should be that of your inner self, the unfading beauty of a gentle and quiet spirit, which is of great worth in God's sight."

God looks at the beauty inside, not what is seen outside. Remember when the prophet Samuel was sent by God to anoint David as king? He met all of David's brothers first, who were a lot taller and of larger stature than David. Samuel was convinced the eldest brother should be anointed. But God says, "Do not consider his appearance or his height, for I have rejected him. The Lord does not look at the things people look at. People look at the outward appearance, but the Lord looks at the heart." (1 Samuel 16:7) Later, King David was described as "a man after God's own heart."

Would the Lord look at your heart today and think it's beautiful? Are you kind? Are you loving? Do you ask God to help you live a life pleasing to him? Do you have compassion for the sick, the poor, the hurting? I may be wrong, but I think that is what God is talking about here. This constitutes beauty to him. We have all known people we did not consider attractive when we first met, but as we got to know their wonderful personalities, they changed into great beauties in our eyes. The same is also true of the flip side. Attractive people become ugly if we discover they are selfish and mean-spirited.

The Bible does talk about a beauty contest in the Old Testament. It is the story of Esther, the orphaned niece of Mordecai, the Jew. She entered a beauty competition to become queen of Persia. The Persians' version of airbrushing was a lot different, and took more time as Esther underwent a year's worth of beauty treatments before the king could lay eyes on her.

Esther eventually won, but in the process, did not reveal her nationality. But make no mistake about it. This story is not about Esther's beauty. It seems King Xerxes eventually became disinterested in Esther, and didn't call for her much. You and I both know that outer beauty only goes so far. No, this story is about Esther's intelligence and her faith. When Esther's uncle, Mordecai, came to her and told her the King had agreed to a plan to execute all the Jews in Persia, Esther became desperate for God. In a nutshell, after much fasting, praying, and dining, Esther revealed to the king that she, his beautiful wife, was a Jew, and thereby slated for execution. Outraged, the king ordered the planner of the anti-Jewish campaign to be executed, and the Jews were saved. Esther's outer beauty may have had something to do with her becoming queen, but it was her inner beauty that pleased the Lord.

Scarf of Truth:
Everything will be beautiful in eternity.

Ecclesiastes 3:11 promises, "He has made everything beautiful in its time. He has also set eternity in the human heart." If God has set eternity in our hearts, then that is where our beauty resides, because in eternity, everything will be beautiful. Revelation describes the New Jerusalem in vivid detail: walls made of jasper, a city of pure gold, the foundations of the city walls decorated with every kind of precious stone. The twelve gates of the city will have twelve gates, each gate made of a single pearl. The great street of the city will be constructed of pure gold. For those of us who love jewelry, that sounds incredibly beautiful, doesn't it? But it's not just the city that will display beauty in eternity; we will also be more beautiful!

In a prophecy about eternity in Zechariah 9:16, the Word gives us this visual: "The LORD their God will save his people on that day as a shepherd saves his flock. They will sparkle in his land like jewels in a crown." Look in the mirror and tell yourself you are like a jewel in a crown! Verse 17 says: "How attractive and beautiful they will be!"

Wow! What a promise to hold on to. Everyone will be beautiful in eternity.

Scarf of Truth:
We must ask God to help us see all his children through his eyes.

We must use God's looking glass to see all his children. If we do, God will provide a different definition for "beautiful." There are two sides to this beauty coin: people who are attractive and people who aren't.

People who aren't attractive by our culture's standards sometimes get shunned, passed over, and neglected. We've all heard the stories of babies who are abandoned because they were born with deformities. We've also all been through junior high and high school, where the unattractive are taunted. Cindy was from a poor family growing up, and was considered unattractive. She remembered how the boys taunted her and how her senior high class voted her "most likely to be an old maid," thereby labeling her as not as valuable as others. Like Cindy, I had my share of teasing in elementary school. Because I was pleasingly plump, my weight didn't lend itself to popularity with the boys.

I remember one boy labeling me "the tank." If I saw him today, I would thank him, because even though his words stung at the time, it was the catalyst I needed to begin exercising and losing my weight in a healthy way. By the time I hit seventh grade, you could call me a "skinny as a rail train," rather than "tank."

On the flipside are people who are physically beautiful. I remember when a very attractive, young news anchor came to work at the television station where I worked as a sportscaster. Very few of the other female news anchors would even speak to her, probably because of their jealousy. Because she was given the cold shoulder, I felt sorry for her, so I made an effort to be nice to her. It was my way of sharing the love of Christ, and I remember I was one of the few on-air females invited to her baby shower. We have to get past our insecurity in this area, and God can help us do this through prayer.

In both cases, we must ask God to lift the veil from our eyes so we can see people the way he does. I think about the blind man in Mark 8:23–25:

> When [Jesus] had spit on the man's eyes and put his hands on him, Jesus asked, "Do you see anything?"
>
> He looked up and said, "I see people; they look like trees walking around."
>
> Once more Jesus put his hands on the man's eyes. Then his eyes were opened, his sight was restored, and he saw everything clearly.

We have scales on our vision when it comes to seeing real beauty. We must allow Jesus to put his hands on us and remove these scales from our spiritual vision so we can see his children through his looking glass.

Scarf of Truth:
God thinks you are beautiful.

Don't you know it's true? Are you looking at yourself with God's looking glass? Or do you look at yourself through the world's tainted, warped, and dirtied lenses?

Rachel, a pretty, petite woman, remembered her struggle with bulimia and her obsession with achieving beauty. The first time she forced herself to throw up, she'd eaten too much at a fast food restaurant. Feeling disgustingly full, she'd read about bulimia in a magazine and thought she'd try it. After throwing up she didn't feel guilt, she felt empowered. This was one way she could have some control over her life. She was hooked and dabbled with bulimia as a novelty in the eighth and ninth grade. Then she moved from Minnesota to Denver, and her need for acceptance took over.

"Pretty was my idol," Rachel said. "Pretty equaled approval. Pretty equaled acceptance. Pretty equaled love. Everything rode on pretty." During this time, she did put on weight, but she thought no one had noticed until one day someone called her fat. "That was it," she said. "I went to full-blown bulimia."

Though Rachel started losing weight and trimmed down to 115, she was still miserable. "I assumed that if I got to 110, everything would be fixed," she said. "Then it became 105, then 100, then 95. If I couldn't get to 95, then I was a failure. I had sores eating up the inside of my mouth . . . sores down my throat making me sick. I had no joy."

Her battle with bulimia continued through high school, college, and into her early married life. Rachel's life spun out of control. "The night before I found out I was pregnant, I went out for Mexican food. I ate too much and made myself sick," Rachel said. The next day, God spoke to her. "I knew I was having a daughter. God told me that if I didn't stop, my daughter would do this, too, and I would have that blood on my hands."

After Rachel gave birth to her daughter and son, she started struggling again. "I was heading down the slope to anorexia." Fortunately, she sensed God speak to her spirit again. "He told me that I couldn't work for him if he wasn't my God," Rachel said. "He also showed me that every idol demands a sacrifice. Christ . . . gives peace, soundness of mind . . . An idol takes it. Finally, he showed me we weren't dealing with an eating disorder; we were dealing with a heart disorder."

That's when Rachel was delivered from her eating disorder. God has now given her a new view of herself. "I want to look like what a woman looks like," Rachel said. "A biblical woman looks like a picture of dignity, serenity, quiet confidence, a good steward of her body."

One of Rachel's beloved Bible verses is Zechariah 2:8: For this is what the LORD Almighty says: "After the Glorious One has sent me against the nations that have plundered you—for whoever touches you touches the apple of his eye. . ."

"I know I'm the apple of his eye," Rachel said. "God is faithful to remind me of it when I forget."

Do you give in to the negative images of yourself? Maybe you had a gawky childhood, like I had. It's over. Perhaps others have been unkind to you about your looks over the years. Forget it. You must see yourself as God sees you. The Lord makes it very clear in Psalm 45:10 when he says: "Royal bride, listen. Think about this and pay attention to it. Forget about your people and the home you came from." (NIrV)

In other words, this passage is saying forget what has happened in the past and what others have said about you. Forget it all. Here's what you need to do when you are feeling insecure about your beauty:

Stop.

Listen.

Go to a quiet place and meditate on God's words to you.

Read the next verse, Psalm 45:11: "The king is charmed by your beauty." (NIrV)

This verse translates in *The Message*: "The King is wild for you!"

God is wild for you, ladies, and thinks you are beautiful. You are, indeed, the apple of his eye.

So which of the two messages will you believe about yourself? The world's message that says you aren't good enough, or God's truth that says you are beautiful. A biblical self-image won't be immediate, but if you pursue his vision you will eventually see yourself and each other through God's looking glass.

Gloves of Prayer: *Lord I am guilty of comparing myself to others rather than being content with the beauty you have given me. Show me how to carry myself with confidence, knowing you created me perfectly. Help me to rest in the fact that I am beautiful in your eyes. Teach me how to be gorgeous on the inside so your beauty will radiate outside to everyone I come in contact with. In Jesus' name, AMEN.*

Discussion Questions:
If I Only Had . . . Beauty

1. Do you believe "If I Only Had . . . Beauty" you'd be more secure?

2. In youth, many of us experienced gawkiness, pop-bottle thick lenses, bad hair years, or erupting faces. Did you have an ugly duckling phase growing up? If so, describe it. How do those messages still repeat themselves in your mind years later?

3. According to photographer and retoucher Tim Lynch, ninety-nine percent of the celebrity photos you see in the media have been altered. How is your sense of beauty affected by our society's airbrushed standards? Do you spend a lot of time and money each day covering up and lifting up that which God made? What part of your outward appearance is hard for you to accept?

4. Comparing ourselves to others is like constantly changing the focus on the camera. To whom do you compare yourself with and, in your mind, do you come up lacking?

5. In Isaiah 53:2 the prophesy about Jesus says, "He had no beauty or majesty to attract us to him, nothing in his appearance that we should desire him." What about Jesus causes you to love and desire him? What is it about other people that attracts you to them? How can you use these insights to change how you feel about your own beauty?

6. In 1 Samuel 16:7 it says, "The Lord does not look at the things people look at. People look at the outward appearance, but

the Lord looks at the heart." What do you think God finds beautiful about your heart?

7. Everything is beautiful in eternity. Imagine how you will look in eternity. Describe yourself. Have fun with this!

8. We diet, we have surgery, we pinch, we prod, sometimes in the name of health and sometimes for beauty. Do you do anything to make yourself more physically attractive that might be displeasing to God?

9. Zechariah 2:8 says, "For this is what the LORD Almighty says: 'After the Glorious One has sent me against the nations that have plundered you—for whoever touches you touches the apple of his eye . . .'" Do you deeply believe that you are the apple of God's eye? Why or why not? Do you pray for his eyes concerning your beauty?

10. In 1 Peter 3:3–4 God outlines that beauty to him comes from the inner self, the "unfading beauty of a gentle and quiet spirit." What can you do to cultivate beauty that is pleasing to God?

Twelve

I Have . . .
A Secure Cornerstone

GROWING UP, MY FAVORITE movie was *The Wizard of Oz*. Well into the years after I graduated from college, I watched this classic every time it aired. As I was thinking about how to wrap up our time together, it occurred to me that our road trip through these pages has been a great deal like the journey Dorothy, The Scarecrow, The Tin Man, and The Cowardly Lion took as they ventured down the yellow brick road. After a tornado plopped her into the Land of Oz, Dorothy simply wanted to return home to Kansas, but the other three were beset by "if onlys." The Tin Man said, "If I only had a heart." The Scarecrow said, "If I only had a brain." The Cowardly Lion said, "If I only had courage."

Those "if onlys" kept them from being who they were created to be. In our case, as we maneuvered down our yellow brick road, our thoughts led us down wrong paths.

"If I only had money in savings."

"If I only looked more gorgeous."

"If I only had a more loving spouse."

"If I'd only had more positive reinforcement as a child."

The characters in the movie all made their journey together, each believing he or she lacked something that would make him or her feel more secure. They shared laughs and tears, fears and excitement as they sought wholeness in their personal lives. I hope you've realized on this journey that like them, you aren't alone on your "yellow brick road." `

Scarf of Truth:
You are not alone in your struggle with insecurity.

Our insecurity is heightened because we mistakenly think other people have it all together. Over the years, hearing other people's stories, I've come to realize they don't. I am often reminded of a story my friend Kayann told me years ago about a couple in her neighborhood who took a weekly walk, holding hands.

This caused some insecurity to arise in her marriage, so Kayann said to her husband, "Why can't you be more loving like him?" Within a month, the hand-holding husband filed for divorce. Kayann realized then that perception and truth are not the same. People's lives are not always what they look like from the outside.

There are countless wounded people in the world, and the testimonies included in these chapters represent a small sample of what is going on globally. Hearing people's stories and being honest about our own stories helps us all feel a little more secure. Remember, everyone has a worldly reason to feel insecure, but also has a Savior who offers us security.

Scarf of Truth:
We already have all we need to be secure.

Security is a beautiful new outfit that Jesus has bought for you. Have you taken it off the hanger and tried it on, or are the moths making a meal out of it? We forget Jesus is the only one who can give us complete security in our lives, and instead we try to find stability in other people or things.

A few years ago, Beth was desperate about the future of her marriage. When she discovered her husband occasionally sent what she considered to be flirtatious emails to female coworkers, she was consumed with insecurity. During this time, she found herself obsessively watching her husband, secretly checking his emails in an attempt to control the situation.

This went on for two years until she realized her actions and words were not making the situation any better. Instead, it was taking her focus away from her ministry activities and the calling Jesus had for her life. Beth concluded only the Holy Spirit could convict her husband about his actions and bring stability into her marriage. After much prayer and surrender, Beth saw her marriage improve, but she also began to draw her security from her faith in Christ rather than her husband.

You are loved by God, and you have the power in Christ to be a secure woman of faith. Jesus went before us, so with Jesus, there is no looking at the past with disappointment. No straining for the future with desperation. There is nothing we can go through he did not endure or does not understand. He set the standard for us on how to be secure, and he's the rock we should set our feet on. With Jesus as our foundation and cornerstone, we can check our "if onlys" at the door!

Scarf of Truth:
Jesus lived and died to be the cornerstone for humankind.

Jesus as the Cornerstone is prophesied in Isaiah 28:16: "So this is what the Sovereign LORD says: 'See, I lay a stone in Zion, a tested stone, a precious cornerstone for a sure foundation; the one who relies on it will never be stricken with panic.'"

This prophecy about Jesus was written about 700 years before the birth of Christ! In the *New Living Translation* of Matthew 21:42, Jesus refers to himself as the cornerstone, tying himself back to the prophecy in Isaiah: "Then Jesus asked them, 'Didn't you ever read this in the Scriptures? 'The stone that the builders rejected has now become the cornerstone. This is the Lord's doing, and it is wonderful to see.'" Jesus was part of God's intricate plan to provide salvation for us by being a living sacrifice, carrying the weight of our sins to the cross. Only the Secure Cornerstone could handle all that weight.

In ancient times, the cornerstone was the stone uniting two walls. It was the most costly stone because of its beauty and strength. The largest, most solid, and most carefully constructed stone, it was the place where the building was joined, and the place where it rested.

From Gill's Exposition of the Bible, "Christ is the sure, firm and everlasting foundation, which God has laid in Zion, and the only one of any avail ... Whoever builds on him are safe, and on nothing else." [1]

One other fact: In ancient times, it was nearly impossible to construct a building without the cornerstone, just as it is impossible for our structure to stand without Jesus as our cornerstone.

Through his teaching here on earth and because of the sacrifice he made on the cross, Jesus is the cornerstone of Christianity. Throughout his three-year ministry in this world, Jesus taught us how to live and love unconditionally; his love is so great he died a brutal death for us. Over the course of history, Christians have been martyred for their beliefs. His strength allowed them to stand strong in their faith, even though it meant an untimely death. We would not be Christ-followers if we didn't believe what took place over 2,000 years ago and did not experience the risen Christ as the cornerstone and foundation of our lives today.

Scarf of Truth:
Our lives must be built with Jesus as our personal cornerstone.

Picture yourself in a boat like the apostles on the Sea of Galilee. The wind is whipping all around you, stirring up the waves. Dark clouds move across the sky. You hear the rumblings of thunder in the distance. You sit, white-knuckled, in your boat, which is named after your predominant insecurity. For some, the boat is named beauty; others name it money; still others call it intelligence. The boat is rocking uncontrollably, sometimes, pitching a little too much in one direction. You hold on to your wooden boat for dear life.

Looking at the safe shore, you see a man walking toward you. You blink your eyes to make sure what you are seeing is real. The vision does not change. Jesus draws closer and asks you to join him for a walk on the water. Do you let your fingers leave the security of the boat and pry them off the wood you're holding? Where does your security lie?

Ellen knew Christ at an early age and always felt he was the cornerstone of her life. "As a younger child, I was very joyful, and I used to sing, 'This Little Light of Mine.' I've always known that Jesus loves me."

Ellen remembered moving from Germany to the United States when she was seven. She had been in school about two weeks and the kids had all included her and treated her nicely. One day it all changed as she looked up and saw two girls pointing at her. Then they began to chant "dirty Nazi kraut." She stood transfixed as a group of boys and girls surrounded her, continuing the chant. Other stood back and watched.

Afraid and confused, Ellen looked to her teacher, pleading with her eyes for help.

Her teacher quickly looked the other way, and then shortly after called the class to go inside, never saying a word.

"After that, no one would speak to me or play with me because if they did, they would be taunted by the 'in crowd,'" Ellen said.

With Christ as her strength, Ellen turned the situation around within a couple of years. "While my classmates stood back, I would always invite the new students to eat lunch with me," Ellen said. Because of her experience, she had compassion for other new kids.

Ellen says she learned early on that you don't wait until a crisis to build a foundation. "You must build it all the time so when a life crisis hits, you don't have to call out for God. He's there; the Holy Spirit is around you, and you feel it." This philosophy carried her through other challenging situations during the course of her life. Ellen says she knew God was holding her hand through two difficult pregnancies, the death of her father, and her husband's decision to deny Christ after twenty-five years of Christian marriage. Three years later, when she discovered her pilot husband was having a long-distance affair, she had immediate peace and confidence that she would be okay. "When I confronted Jim about the affair three weeks after I had found out, I knew I already forgave him."

After admitting to multiple infidelities and financial deceptions, Ellen's husband eventually divorced her. "He asked me if he had broken my heart when he said he no longer believed in Christ. I said, 'No, because my heart belongs to Christ.'" She is not bitter about what has happened, but resolute that God has a plan for her future. "That's because I have that foundation. He built me the way I am."

Jesus is Ellen's secure cornerstone.

Scarf of Truth:
When we rely on Jesus as our cornerstone, our personal walls cannot be shaken.

The Biblical example that keeps coming back to me is the Apostle Paul. Like many in our culture, Paul thought he had it all together before his encounter with Christ. He was an up-and-coming leader in the Jewish faith. In Philippians 3:5–6, Paul lists his worldly accomplishments: "circumcised on the eighth day, of the people of Israel, of the tribe of Benjamin, a Hebrew of Hebrew; in regard to the law, a Pharisee, as for zeal, persecuting the church; as for legalistic righteousness based on the law, faultless."

But despite his sparkling resume, Paul's walls were shaken on the road to Damascus. He was blinded and weakened because the foundation he had built his life on did not have Jesus as his cornerstone. Later, when speaking to the Corinthians, Paul said in 1 Corinthians 3:10–11: "By the grace God has given me, I laid a foundation as a wise builder, and someone else is building on it. But each one should build with care. For no one can lay any foundation other than the one already laid, which is Jesus Christ."

Here's a question for you. Are you the one making the decisions about what is built on your foundation, or are you letting Christ be your building foreman?

Did the troubles stop for Paul once he became a Christian? We all know the answer to that is no. He gives a synopsis of his woes in 2 Corinthians 11:25–27:

Three times I was beaten with rods, once I was pelted with stones, three times I was shipwrecked, I spent a night and a day in the open sea, I have been constantly on the move. I have been in danger from rivers, in danger from bandits, in danger from my fellow Jews, in danger from Gentiles; in danger in the city, in danger in the country, in danger at sea; and in danger from false believers. I have labored and toiled and have often gone without sleep; I have known hunger and thirst and have often gone without food; I have been cold and naked.

But through all this, Paul's personal walls were not shaken. Paul's problems make my problems seem insignificant.

When I start my day laying a foundation with the Lord, I know that whatever comes my way is of him, and he will guide me through it. That's how Paul endured all his troubles. That's how Paul could rejoice always. That's how he could pray without ceasing. That is how the perseverant Paul trudged on in his missionary work despite extreme persecution and danger, sharing the Gospel everywhere he traveled. Paul's personal walls were not shaken, and we can claim that kind of victory, as well, with Christ as our cornerstone.

I admit that during some of the most difficult stretches of my life, I was not as close to Christ as I should have been. However, when I was walking more faithfully, surrendering to Jesus daily, my problems didn't seem as troublesome because I rested on the foundation of Christ.

Years ago, when I was denied renewal on two television contracts in the same week, I was a mess. I went from two cushy jobs on national television and a regional cable network to nothing, practically overnight. Questioning God about it, I pestered my agent daily and complained to my husband 24/7. Because I did not have a strong foundation to stand on, I never rested in what turned out to be six months off from work. Not being secure in my situation, I didn't realize the Lord had his hand in this all along. He was using this devastation to draw me back to him and rebuild my life with Jesus as my cornerstone, because my walls were crumbling without him. Here's an "if only" for you . . . if only I had trusted my Lord and Savior during this time.

After I rededicated my life to Christ, God gave me seven more years in television. When I determined it was time to leave broadcasting for good, I handled it much differently. In the midst of a difficult time, I trusted God with where he would lead me, and because my life was built on Jesus as my Cornerstone and centered around God, I was secure in the situation.

Scarf of Truth:
With Jesus as our cornerstone, God's armor is at our fingertips.

Satan could not shake the Apostle Paul's faith because he never took his eyes off Christ. Yes, Paul admits his weakness numerous times. Paul reminds the Corinthians in 2 Corinthians 13:4: "For to be sure, he was crucified in weakness, yet he lives by God's power. Likewise, we are weak in him, yet by God's power we will live with him in our dealing with you." Paul was very aware of the evil forces around us that attempt to tear down our walls, so in Ephesians 6:10–18, he gives us the formula for overcoming, and he calls it "the armor of God." Many of us have heard this before, but we don't always put it into practice. As you read through it again, note how he is giving you the guideline for being totally secure in Christ.

Finally, be strong in the Lord and in his mighty power. Put on the full armor of God, so that you can take your stand against the devil's schemes. For our struggle is not against flesh and blood, but against the rulers, against the authorities, against the powers of this dark world and against the spiritual forces of evil in the heavenly realms. Therefore put on the full armor of God, so that when the day of evil comes, you may be able to stand your ground, and after you have done everything, to stand. Stand firm then, with the belt of truth buckled around your waist, with the breastplate of righteousness in place, and with your feet fitted with the readiness that comes from the gospel of peace. In addition to all this, take up the shield of faith, with which you can extinguish all the flaming arrows of the evil one. Take the helmet of salvation and the sword of the Spirit, which is the word of God.

And pray in the Spirit on all occasions with all kinds of prayers and requests. With this in mind, be alert and always keep on praying for all the Lord's people.

Paul used armor to talk about our relationship to God because armored soldiers were familiar fixtures for his audience. But for us, ladies, let's mix it up a bit with a more modern, feminine version of putting on the full armor of God. Let us prepare for the storms of our lives with the appropriate bad weather attire.

We already introduced you to the **scarves of truth** and **gloves of prayer** and hope you've been using them throughout the reading of *If I Only Had* ... Wrapping yourselves in truth and sliding on God's gloves of prayers are two important ways to stave off the thunderstorms of life, but protection from storms wouldn't be complete without opening up our **umbrella of faith**.

An umbrella's job is to protect us from pelting rain. We use our umbrella of faith to stop the cold, driving shower that comes suddenly, often at times and from places we don't expect. Call it a surprise thunderstorm. Our umbrella of faith is, as Hebrews 11:1 says, "confidence in what we hope for and assurance about what we do not see."

Using our umbrella, we see our lives more clearly because it shields our eyes from the driving rain. Our umbrella of faith gives us a heavenly perspective as we walk through the storm. God wants us to see material things, our appearance, and relationships, things we thought would make us secure, from his point of view. In this book, we have unveiled God's clear vision on the "if onlys" in our lives:

Striving for intelligence transforms into praying for Godly wisdom.

Competing for outer attractiveness becomes yearning for inner beauty.

Straining for money to feel secure converts to using money to build his kingdom.

Resenting our dysfunctional family turns into being God messenger sent out to share his love and forgiveness.

Attempting to fix those around us morphs into relying on God to be our perfect *Ish*.

Worrying and fretting over the future transforms into opening our hearts to God's plan for our lives.

After we grab our umbrella of faith, we must pull on our **raincoat of righteousness.**

The raincoat defends the heart and represents being in a right relationship with God. Integrity, purity of life, holiness—they are all woven together to make a cloth capable of protecting ourselves from the assaults of Satan. Do we strive for righteousness? Do we desire to be women of integrity? Do we ask the Lord to purify us each day and make us holy? Our raincoat of righteousness protects us from the enemy.

Let's not forget to pull **God's galoshes** onto our feet. God's galoshes represent a firm commitment to what we say we believe. It is the resolve to stand firm in our belief in Jesus and to trust God with what we do not understand.

There is nothing worse than soaking wet feet to dampen our spirit. Galoshes are a layer of protection from the muck and mud of life. With God's galoshes, we can plant ourselves in the truths of the Gospel. No slipping or sliding down the perilous slopes of sin and fear; these galoshes are deeply treaded to assist in traction. They allow us to either stand firm or spring into action when God calls.

At the very top of our bodies is an adorning **holy hat,** our crowning glory of salvation.

A hat insulates our head from rain and cold. This hat is a royal hat because our salvation makes us princesses, doesn't it? When we accept Christ, we are daughters of the King, assured of eternity living with our Father. What would we do without our holy hat of salvation?

Last but not least, we can't run out without our **handbag of the Spirit**.

It is the Word of God carried with us and spoken with the power of the Holy Spirit. Purses hold items for emergencies, even items that can be used as weapons. We've all seen video of a woman hitting a potential assailant with her purse and preventing a crime. Carry a pocket Bible or have a version of the Bible on your phone in your handbag of the Spirit. Use his wordy weapons to beat off an enemy attack. When Christ was tempted by the devil in the wilderness, he countered the temptation with Scripture each time. We can follow his lead with our handbag of the Spirit.

There we have it—our version of the full armor of God to protect us from the storms of our lives: a scarf of truth, gloves of prayer, an umbrella of faith, the raincoat of righteousness, God's galoshes, a holy hat, a handbag of the Spirit, and don't forget to top the whole outfit off with a beautiful strand of heavenly pearls of wisdom.

Scarf of Truth:
With Jesus as our cornerstone, we have hope.

We can find hope in Ephesians 2:19–21: "Consequently, you are no longer foreigners and strangers, but fellow citizens with God's people and also members of his household, built on the foundation of the apostles and prophets, with Christ Jesus himself as the chief cornerstone. In him the whole building is joined together and rises to become a holy temple in the Lord."

Anything made by man is destructible. We have seen this with the unsinkable Titanic going to its watery grave and the symbols of strength and man's ingenuity, the Twin Towers, collapsing after being hit by two planes. But with Jesus as our secure cornerstone, we are a building that is indestructible.

Whether you like to think of yourself as a rock with many cracks and holes or an old house that needs rewiring, remember Jesus, the Great Carpenter, is at work on you. He is remaking us, as it says in 2 Corinthians 5:17: "Therefore, if anyone is in Christ, the new creation has come: The old has gone, the new is here!"

Jesus is our hope! No matter how messy our lives are, no matter what we've been through, if we allow it, his building project on our lives is always a work in progress. Our hope is that one day, because we have the power of Christ within us, we will be perfect and live eternally with God the Father in heaven.

After many detours, Dorothy and her crew finally made it to Oz. Eventually, seeing the Wizard himself, what did they find out? They all realized they had possessed all along what they thought they lacked. Dorothy's answer was always right at her feet. How had she missed it? She was wearing the magical red slippers. Three clicks of her heels, and she would be home again in Kansas!

So it is with us. We've had a lot of detours on our road to security, haven't we? For many of us, our travel has stretched over many years, but now, at long last, we've arrived at our destination where we realize we've had the foundation to be secure all along. For us, the answer is not on our feet; it is close by, in our hearts, where Jesus resides.

Through trial and error, we tried aimlessly to find our security in our mothers or fathers, sisters or brothers, husbands, children, or friends, only to realize they couldn't fill the void in our lives and could not provide our secure foundation. Just as Dorothy had the power to get home by clicking her heels and repeating, "There's no place like home," we have the power through Christ to overcome our weaknesses. Instead of saying, *If I only had . . .* , it is my prayer we've come to the place where we proclaim to Jesus, *You are all I need. You are my rock and my stability. You are my secure cornerstone. There's no one like Jesus; there's no one like Jesus; there's no one like Jesus.*

Gloves of Prayer: *Abba Father, the walls of my life have been unstable because I have not asked Jesus to be my cornerstone. I ask you, Jesus, to become the foundation of my life and rebuild my walls so I will be a secure woman again with you at the center. I know I am weak, but you are strong. I pray I will always put on your protective wear, your scarf of truth, gloves of prayer, umbrella of* faith, raincoat of righteousness, God's galoshes, holy hat, and handbag of the Spirit so I will always be protected when a storm of insecurity blows into my life. In the name above all names, Jesus, AMEN.

Discussion Questions:
I Have . . . a Secure Cornerstone

1. Which chapter in this book best sums up your biggest struggle with insecurity? Does it help to realize you are not alone in your struggle?

2. Security is a beautiful new outfit Jesus has bought for you. Have you taken it off the hanger and tried it on, or are the moths making a meal of it? Do you believe you already have all you need to be secure? Why or why not?

3. In ancient times, the cornerstone was the place where building walls joined, and rested. Jesus lived and died to be the cornerstone for humankind. "See, I lay a stone in Zion, a tested stone, a precious cornerstone for a sure foundation; the one who relies on it will never be stricken with panic." (Isaiah 28:16) How does knowing this change your view of all the wobbly cornerstones the world chases after?

4. When we rely on Jesus as our cornerstone, our personal walls cannot be shaken. Have you ever had your personal walls shaken? What occurred? Knowing what you know now, will you handle challenges differently next time?

5. If we start our day laying a foundation with the Lord, we know that whatever comes our way is of him, and he will guide us through it. What are ways you can make Jesus the foundation of your life?

6. Peter left the safety of the boat and joined Jesus walking on the Sea of Galilee. When you pictured yourself in the boat, what name did you give your boat? With the storm raging,

and Jesus asking you to join him, did you hesitate to leave the boat? What was your hesitation?

7. "Finally, be strong in the Lord and in his mighty power. Put on the full armor of God, so that you can take your stand against the devil's schemes." Read the rest of Ephesians 6:10–18, then re-read our version of the armor of God. Which piece of the bad weather attire are you missing in your life? How will you go about adding it to your spiritual wardrobe?

8. Jesus is our hope! No matter how messy our lives are, no matter what we've been through, his building project in our lives is always a work in progress. How does having Jesus as your cornerstone bring you hope for the future?

9. If you have tried to find stability in other people or things, how can you practically wrap the scarves of truths around you and firmly stand on the truth of God's Word? Which Scripture quoted in this chapter speaks to you the most?

10. Most of us have had plenty of detours on our road to security. How has reading this book helped you start down the road of basing your security on Christ, the secure cornerstone?

Notes

CHAPTER 1: IF I ONLY HAD . . . MORE CONFIDENCE
SCARVES OF TRUTH

- God knows our potential, even if we don't.
- The Lord is with us, even when we lack confidence.
- It may take many encounters with God to overcome insecurity.
- In order to overcome insecurity, we must believe what God says about us.
- God doesn't always fight our battles in the way we imagine he will.

HANDBAG OF THE SPIRIT

Isaiah 64:8: "Yet you, LORD, are our Father. We are the clay, you are the potter; we are all the work of your hand."

John 1:12: "Yet to all who received him, to those who believed in his name, he gave the right to become children of God—"

Jeremiah 1:5: "Before I formed you in the womb I knew you, before you were born I set you apart."

Ephesians 2:10: "For we are God's handiwork, created in Christ Jesus to do good works, which God prepared in advance for us to do."

Proverbs 3:26 from *New King James Version:* "For the LORD will be your confidence, and will keep your foot from being caught."

Isaiah 40:31: "But those who hope in the LORD will renew their strength. They will soar on wings like eagles; they will run

---

and not grow weary, they will walk and not be faint."

Isaiah 43:2: "When you pass through the waters, I will be with you; and when you pass through the rivers, they will not sweep over you. When you walk through the fire, you will not be burned; the flames will not set you ablaze."

Hebrews 10:35–36: "So do not throw away your confidence; it will be richly rewarded. You need to persevere so that when you have done the will of God, you will receive what he has promised."

CHAPTER 2: IF I ONLY HAD . . . HEALTHY THOUGHTS
SCARVES OF TRUTH

- Our thoughts and God's thoughts do not always sync up.
- Sometimes we need to change our surroundings in order to change our thinking.
- When we finally acknowledge God's truths about our life, he will rescue us from our negative thoughts and insecurity.
- God will give us more opportunities to think rightly.
- We must keep our focus on God to keep the negative thoughts from returning.
- When we take our minds off ourselves, and remain focused on God, we are better able to see his bigger picture.

HANDBAG OF THE SPIRIT

Matthew 6:34: "Therefore do not worry about tomorrow, for tomorrow will worry about itself. Each day has enough trouble of its own."

James 1:2–3: "Consider it pure joy, my brothers and sisters, whenever you face trials of many kinds, because you know that the testing of your faith produces perseverance."

Psalm 139:23–24: "Search me, O God, and know my heart; test me and know my anxious thoughts. See if there is any offensive way in me, and lead me in the way everlasting."

Psalm 119:105: "Your word is a lamp for my feet, a light on my path."

Philippians 4:8: "Finally brothers and sisters, whatever is true, whatever is noble, whatever is right, whatever is pure, whatever is lovely, whatever is admirable—if anything is excellent or praiseworthy—think about such things."

Psalm 94:11: "The Lord knows all human plans; he knows that they are futile."

Romans 12:1–2: "Therefore, I urge you, brothers and sisters, in view of God's mercy, to offer your bodies as a living sacrifice, holy and pleasing to God—this is your true and proper worship. Do not conform to the pattern of this world, but be transformed by the renewing of your mind. Then you will be able to test and approve what God's will is—his good, pleasing and perfect will."

2 Corinthians 10:5: "We demolish arguments and every pretension that sets itself up against the knowledge of God, and we take captive every thought to make it obedient to Christ."

CHAPTER 3: IF I ONLY HAD . . . PEACE
SCARVES OF TRUTH

- Fear feeds our insecurity.
- Many times, God reveals his plan for our lives in the unknown.
- Anything can become an idol when it takes God's place, even fear.
- On the path to peace, God will guide us every step of the way, one step at a time.
- On the path to peace, our fear lessens to the degree we know God, choose to trust him, and believe he can heal us.
- Having faith in God and in his Word can protect us from fearful thoughts.
- Perfect love casts out fear.

HANDBAG OF THE SPIRIT

2 Timothy 1:7 from *New King James Version*: "For God has not given us a spirit of fear, but of power and of love and of a sound mind."

Exodus 20:4–5: "You shall not make for yourself an image in the form of anything in heaven above or on the earth beneath or in the waters below. You shall not bow down to them or worship them; . . ."

Psalm 56:3: "When I am afraid, I put my trust in you."

1 Peter 5:8: "Be alert and of sober mind. Your enemy the devil prowls around like a roaring lion looking for someone to devour."

Ephesians 6:16: "In addition to all this, take up the shield of faith, with which you can extinguish all the flaming arrows of the evil one."

Genesis 15:1: "Do not be afraid, Abram. I am your shield, . . ."

Psalm 27:1: "The Lord is my light and my salvation—whom shall I fear?"

Psalm 56:11: "In God I trust and am not afraid. What can man do to me?"

Proverbs 4:23: "Above all else, guard your heart, for everything you do flows from it."

Philippians 4:13: "I can do all this through him who gives me strength."

2 Timothy 1:7: "For the Spirit God gave us does not make us timid, but gives us power, love and self-discipline."

Philippians 4:6: "Do not be anxious about anything, but in every situation, by prayer and petition, with thanksgiving, present your requests to God."

Psalm 34:4: "I sought the LORD, and he answered me; he delivered me from all my fears."

1 John 4:18 from *New King James Version:* "There is no fear in love; but perfect love casts out fear: because fear has torment. But he who fears has not been made perfect in love."

Chapter 4: If I Only Had . . . Dignity
Scarves of Truth

- When we lose our dignity, we should reach out to Jesus first, not last.
- Jesus has the ability to heal us from our illnesses.
- When we feel alone and isolated, Jesus can give us hope.
- Jesus wants to reach out and touch everyone.
- If God is to restore our dignity and provide healing, we must be transparent before him.
- We are all daughters of God.
- It takes faith to regain our dignity and receive healing.

Handbag of the Spirit

Luke 8:46–48: "But Jesus said, 'Someone touched me; I know that power has gone out from me.'

Then the woman, seeing that she could not go unnoticed, came trembling and fell at his feet. In the presence of all the people, she told why she had touched him and how she had been instantly healed. Then he said to her, 'Daughter, your faith has healed you. Go in peace.'"

Matthew 9:10–12: "While Jesus was having dinner at Matthew's house, many tax collectors and sinners came and ate with him and his disciples. When the Pharisees saw this, they asked his disciples, 'Why does your teacher eat with tax collectors and sinners?'

"On hearing this, Jesus said, 'It is not the healthy who need a doctor, but the sick. But go and learn what this means: 'I desire mercy, not sacrifice.' For I have not come to call the righteous, but sinners.'"

John 1:12–13: "Yet to all who did receive him, to those who believed in his name, he gave the right to become children of God—children born not of natural descent, nor of human decision or a husband's will, but born of God."

Proverbs 31:25: "She is clothed with strength and dignity; she can laugh at the days to come."

Genesis 1:27: "So God created mankind in his own image, in the image of God he created them; male and female he created them."

Acts 10:43: "All the prophets testify about him that everyone who believes in him receives forgiveness of sins through his name."

Luke 23:43: "Jesus answered him, 'Truly I tell you, today you will be with me in paradise.'"

CHAPTER 5: IF I ONLY HAD ... A BRAIN
SCARVES OF TRUTH

- We are all intelligent in different ways, according to our God-given talents.
- Wisdom is not the same as intelligence.
- Wisdom is birthed through a healthy fear of the Lord.
- God will give you wisdom if you seek it.
- Our wisdom grows by continually filling ourselves with God's wisdom.
- Our wisdom increases when we wholeheartedly trust in the Lord rather than rely on our own understanding.
- God's wisdom working in our life will make us more like Christ.

HANDBAG OF THE SPIRIT

Exodus 31:1–6: "Then the LORD said to Moses, 'See, I have chosen Bezalel son of Uri, the son of Hur, of the tribe of Judah, and I have filled him with the Spirit of God, with wisdom, with understanding, with knowledge and with all kinds of skills— to make artistic designs for work in gold, silver and bronze, to cut and set stones, to work in wood, and to engage in all kinds of crafts. Moreover, I have appointed

Oholiab son of Ahisamak, of the tribe of Dan, to help him. Also I have given ability to all the skilled workers to make everything I have commanded you: . . . '"

Psalm 111:10: "The fear of The Lord is the beginning of wisdom; all who follow his precepts have good understanding."

Isaiah 33:6: "He will be the sure foundation for your times, a rich store of salvation and wisdom and knowledge; the fear of the LORD is the key to this treasure."

Proverbs 8:13: "To fear the LORD is to hate evil; I hate pride and arrogance, evil behavior and perverse speech."

1 Kings 3:9: "So give your servant a discerning heart to govern your people and to distinguish between right and wrong. For who is able to govern this great people of yours?"

1 Kings 3:12: "I will do what you have asked. I will give you a wise and discerning heart, so that there will never have been anyone like you, nor will there ever be."

Proverbs 2:1–5: "My son, if you accept my words and store up my commands within you, turning your ear to wisdom and applying your heart to understanding—indeed, if you call out for insight and cry aloud for understanding, and if you look for it as for silver and search for it as for hidden treasure, then you will understand the fear of the LORD and find the knowledge of God."

Proverbs 3:5–6: "Trust in the LORD with all your heart and lean not on your own understanding; in all your ways submit to him, and he will make your paths straight."

Proverbs 20:12: "Ears that hear and eyes that see—the LORD has made them both."

Psalm 37:30: "The mouths of the righteous utter wisdom, and their tongues speak what is just."

Ephesians 4:29: "Do not let any unwholesome talk come out of your mouths, but only what is helpful for building others up according to their needs, that it may benefit those who listen."

James 1:26: "Those who consider themselves religious and yet do not keep a tight rein on their tongues deceive themselves, and their religion is worthless."

Matthew 11:19: "The Son of Man came eating and drinking, and they say, "Here is a glutton and a drunkard, a friend of tax collectors and sinners." But wisdom is proved right by her deeds."

CHAPTER 6: IF I ONLY HAD . . . A NORMAL FAMILY
SCARVES OF TRUTH

- Dysfunction happens in the best of families.
- The sins of parents always affect their children.
- Time does not heal all wounds. We must face our family issues.
- God works good out of our trials.
- As we recover from our family dysfunction, God provides new family members through the body of Christ.

HANDBAG OF THE SPIRIT

2 Samuel 11:4–5: "Then David sent messengers to get her. She came to him, and he slept with her. (Now she was purifying herself from her monthly uncleanness.) Then she went back home. The woman conceived and sent word to David, saying, 'I am pregnant.'"

John 5:7–9: "'I have no one to help me into the pool when the water is stirred. While I am trying to get in, someone else goes down ahead of me.' Then Jesus said to him, 'Get up! Pick up your mat and walk.' At once the man was cured; he picked up his mat and walked."

Ephesians 5:11: "Have nothing to do with the fruitless deeds of darkness, but rather expose them."

Romans 8:28: "And we know that in all things God works for the good of those who love him, who have been called according to his purpose."

Matthew 12:50: "For whoever does the will of my Father in heaven
is my brother and sister and mother."

Matthew 6:14–16: "For if you forgive other people when they sin
against you, your heavenly Father will also forgive you. But if
you do not forgive others their sins, your Father will not forgive your sins."

Psalm 145:4: "One generation commends your works to another,
they tell of your mighty acts."

Hebrews 11:1: "Now faith is confidence in what we hope for and
assurance about what we do not see."

Romans 8:28: "And we know that in all things God works for the
good of those who love him, who have been called according to his purpose."

CHAPTER 7: IF I ONLY HAD . . . A BETTER MARRIAGE
SCARVES OF TRUTH

- Only God can fix your man!
- Our spouses will never make us 100 percent secure in our
  marriages.
- Seven Reasons God is the Perfect *Ish* (Husband):
  1. God is never too busy for us.
  2. God listens to us.
  3. God encourages us.
  4. God is content with us.
  5. God protects us.
  6. God loves us.
  7. God will never abandon us.

HANDBAG OF THE SPIRIT

Isaiah 54:5–8: "'For your Maker is your husband (ISH) —the Lord
Almighty is His name—the Holy One of Israel is your
Redeemer; he is called the God of all the earth. The LORD
will call you back as if you were a wife deserted and

distressed in spirit—a wife who married young, only to be rejected,' says your God. 'For a brief moment I abandoned you, but with deep compassion I will bring you back. In a surge of anger I hid my face from you for a moment but with everlasting kindness I will have compassion on you,' says the LORD your Redeemer."

Psalm 121:5–8: "The Lord watches over you—the Lord is your shade at your right hand; the sun will not harm you by day, nor the moon by night. The Lord will keep you from all harm—he will watch over your life; the Lord will watch over your coming and going both now and forevermore."

2 Kings 20:5: "This is what the LORD, the God of your father David, says: I have heard your prayer and seen your tears; I will heal you."

Revelation 5:8: "Each one had a harp and they were holding golden bowls full of incense, which are the prayers of God's people."

1 Peter 3:8–9: "Finally, all of you, be like-minded, be sympathetic, love one another, be compassionate and humble. Do not repay evil with evil or insult with insult. On the contrary, repay evil with blessing, because to this you were called so that you may inherit a blessing."

Psalm 139:13: "For you created my inmost being; you knit me together in my mother's womb."

Psalm 91:9–14: "If you say, 'The LORD is my refuge,' and you make the Most High your dwelling, no harm will overtake you, no disaster will come near your tent. For he will command his angels concerning you to guard you in all your ways; they will lift you up in their hands, so that you will not strike your foot against a stone. You will tread on the lion and the cobra; you will trample the great lion and the serpent. 'Because he loves me,' says the LORD, 'I will rescue him; I will protect him, for he acknowledges my name.'"

Romans 5:6–8: "You see, at just the right time, when we were still powerless, Christ died for the ungodly. Very rarely will anyone die for a righteous person, though for a good person someone might possibly dare to die. But God demonstrates his own love for us in this: While we were still sinners, Christ died for us."

Matthew 6:34: "Therefore do not worry about tomorrow, for tomorrow will worry about itself. Each day has enough trouble of its own."

Deuteronomy 31:8: "The LORD himself goes before you and will be with you; he will never leave you nor forsake you. Do not be afraid; do not be discouraged."

CHAPTER 8: IF I ONLY HAD . . . A CHILD
SCARVES OF TRUTH

- God understands barrenness.
- Being barren is not a punishment from God.
- God is sovereign.
- Security is a fruit of accepting God's plan for your life.
- Oftentimes, God answers our prayers for a child.
- Let God open your heart to his possibilities.
- Follow God's call to be a spiritual mother.
- We learn from God during the barren times.

HANDBAG OF THE SPIRIT

1 Samuel 1:8: "Her husband Elkanah would say to her, 'Hannah, why are you weeping? Why don't you eat? Why are you downhearted? Don't I mean more to you than ten sons?'"

Job 31:5–6: "If I have walked with falsehood or my foot has hurried after deceit—let God weigh me in honest scales and he will know that I am blameless . . ."

1 John 1:9: "If we confess our sins, he is faithful and just and will forgive us our sins and purify us from all unrighteousness."

Luke 15:22–24: "But the father said to his servants, 'Quick! Bring the best robe and put it on him. Put a ring on his finger and sandals on his feet. Bring the fattened calf and kill it. Let's have a feast and celebrate. For this son of mine was dead and is alive again; he was lost and is found.' So they began to celebrate."

Job 38:4–7: "Where were you when I laid the earth's foundation? Tell me, if you understand. Who marked off its dimensions? Surely you know! Who stretched a measuring line across it? On what were its footings set, or who laid its cornerstone while the morning stars sang together and all the angels shouted for joy?"

Job 42:1–3: "Then Job replied to the Lord: 'I know that you can do all things; no purpose of yours can be thwarted. You asked, 'Who is this that obscures my plans without knowledge?' Surely I spoke of things I did not understand, things too wonderful for me to know."

1 Samuel 1:11: "And she made a vow, saying, 'LORD Almighty, if you will only look on your servant's misery and remember me, and not forget your servant but give her a son, then I will give him to the LORD for all the days of his life, and no razor will ever be used on his head.'"

1 Samuel 1:15–16: "'Not so, my lord,' Hannah replied, 'I am a woman who is deeply troubled. I have not been drinking wine or beer; I was pouring out my soul to the LORD. Do not take your servant for a wicked woman; I have been praying here out of my great anguish and grief.'"

Jeremiah 29:11: "For I know the plans I have for you, declares the Lord, plans to prosper you and not to harm you, plans to give you hope and a future."

Titus 2:4–5: "Then they [the older women] can urge the younger women to love their husbands and children, to be self-controlled and pure, to be busy at home, to be kind, and to be subject to their husbands, so that no one will malign the word of God."

Psalm 113:9: "He settles the childless woman in her home as a happy mother of children."

Matthew 11:28–30: "Come to me, all you who are weary and burdened, and I will give you rest. Take my yoke upon you and learn from me, for I am gentle and humble in heart, and you will find rest for your souls. For my yoke is easy and my burden is light."

Philippians 4:19: "And my God will meet all your needs according to the riches of his glory in Christ Jesus."

CHAPTER 9: IF I ONLY HAD . . . CLOSER FRIENDSHIPS
SCARVES OF TRUTH
- Forced friendships don't work, and can heighten insecurity.
- Room: Give friends room to mess up.
- Insecurity in friendships often starts with you!
- Encouraging friends and being honest draws friends closer.
- Never be too busy for your friends.
- Divine bonds are powerful in friendships.

HANDBAG OF THE SPIRIT
Proverbs 27:6: "Wounds from a friend can be trusted, but an enemy multiplies kisses."

Proverbs 17:17: "A friend loves at all times . . ."

Matthew 5:39: "If anyone slaps you on the right cheek, turn to them the other cheek also."

Luke 19:5–6: "When Jesus reached the spot, he looked up and said to him, 'Zacchaeus, come down immediately. I must stay at your house today.' So he came down at once and welcomed Him gladly."

1 Thessalonians 5:11: "Therefore encourage one another and build each other up, just as in fact you are doing."

John 16:33: "I have told you these things, so that in me you may
    have peace. In this world you will have trouble. But take
    heart! I have overcome the world."
Proverbs 27:17: "As iron sharpens iron, so one person sharpens
    another."
Matthew 16:22–23: "Peter took him aside and began to rebuke
    him. 'Never, Lord!' he said. 'This shall never happen to you!'
        "Jesus turned and said to Peter, 'Get behind me, Satan!
    You are a stumbling block to me; you do not have in mind
    the things of God, but merely human concerns.'"
Matthew 10:39: "Whoever finds their life will lose it, and whoever
    loses their life for my sake will find it."
Proverbs 18:24: "One who has unreliable friends soon comes to
    ruin, but there is a friend who sticks closer than a brother."
1 Samuel 18:1: "After David had finished talking with Saul,
    Jonathan became one in spirit with David, and he loved
    him as himself."
John 15:12: "My command is this: Love each other as I have loved
    you."

CHAPTER 10: IF I ONLY HAD . . . MORE MONEY
SCARVES OF TRUTH

- God uses money as a barometer of our heart condition.
- God often uses money problems to redirect our lives.
- Money is not the answer to our problems. God is.
- God wants us to give others access to our excess.
- Money should never influence how we treat others.
- Money should be used for eternal purposes.

HANDBAG OF THE SPIRIT

Matthew 6:21: "For where your treasure is, there your heart will be
    also."
Mark 10:21–22 from *The Message:* "Jesus looked him hard in the

eye—and loved him! He said, 'There's one thing left: Go sell whatever you own and give it to the poor. All your wealth will then be heavenly wealth. And come follow me.'"

"The man's face clouded over. This was the last thing he expected to hear, and he walked off with a heavy heart. He was holding on tight to a lot of things, and not about to let go."

Proverbs 1:19: "Such are the paths of all who go after ill-gotten gain; it takes away the life of those who get it."

Proverbs 11:28: "Those who trust in their riches will fall, but the righteous will thrive like a green leaf."

Proverbs 16:8: "Better a little with righteousness than much gain with injustice."

Ecclesiastes 2:10–11: "I denied myself nothing my eyes desired; I refused my heart no pleasure. My heart took delight in all my labor, and this was the reward for all my toil. Yet when I surveyed all that my hands had done and what I had toiled to achieve, everything was meaningless, a chasing after the wind; nothing was gained under the sun."

Malachi 3:10: "'Bring the whole tithe into the storehouse, that there may be food in my house. Test me in this,' says the LORD Almighty, 'and see if I will not throw open the floodgates of heaven and pour out so much blessing that there will not be room enough to store it.'"

Acts 4:32: "All the believers were one in heart and mind. No one claimed that any of their possessions was their own, but they shared everything they had."

James 5:1–5 from *The Message*: "And a final word to you arrogant rich: Take some lessons in lament. You'll need buckets for the tears when the crash comes upon you. Your money is corrupt and your fine clothes stink. Your greedy luxuries are a cancer in your gut, destroying your life from within. You thought you were piling up wealth. What you've piled up is judgment. All the workers you've exploited and cheated cry out for judgment. The groans of the workers you used and abused are a roar in the ears of the Master Avenger."

Mathew 25:40: "The King will reply, 'Truly I tell you, whatever you did for one of the least of these brothers and sisters of mine, you did for me.'"

Matthew 6:19–21: "Do not store up for yourselves treasures on earth, where moths and vermin destroy and where thieves break in and steal. But store up for yourselves treasures in heaven, where moths and vermin do not destroy, and where thieves do not break in and steal. For where your treasure is, there your heart will be also."

CHAPTER 11: IF I ONLY HAD . . . BEAUTY
SCARVES OF TRUTH

- When it comes to beauty, we often look at ourselves under a magnifying glass.
- Our sense of personal beauty can't be defined by our society's airbrushed standards.
- We will be more secure if we don't compare ourselves to others.
- To understand what real beauty is, we must consult the Bible.
- Everything will be beautiful in eternity.
- We must ask God to help us see all his children through his eyes.
- God thinks you are beautiful.

HANDBAG OF THE SPIRIT

Isaiah 53:2: "He grew up before him like a tender shoot, and like a root out of dry ground. He had no beauty or majesty to attract us to him, nothing in his appearance that we should desire him."

Psalm 139:15–16: "My frame was not hidden from you when I was made in the secret place, when I was woven together in the depths of the earth. Your eyes saw my unformed body; all the days ordained for me were written in your book before one of them came to be."

1 Peter 3:3–4: "Your beauty should not come from outward adornment, such as elaborate hairstyles and the wearing of gold jewelry or fine clothes. Rather, it should be that of your inner self, the unfading beauty of a gentle and quiet spirit, which is of great worth in God's sight."

1 Samuel 16:7: "But the Lord said to Samuel, 'Do not consider his appearance or his height, for I have rejected him. The Lord does not look at the things people look at. People look at the outward appearance, but the Lord looks at the heart.'"

Ecclesiastes 3:11: "He has made everything beautiful in its time. He has also set eternity in the human heart."

Zechariah 9:16–17: "The LORD their God will save his people on that day as a shepherd saves his flock. They will sparkle in his land like jewels in a crown. How attractive and beautiful they will be!"

Mark 8:23–25: "When [Jesus] had spit on the man's eyes and put his hands on him, Jesus asked, 'Do you see anything?' He looked up and said, 'I see people; they look like trees walking around.' Once more Jesus put his hands on the man's eyes. Then his eyes were opened, his sight was restored, and he saw everything clearly."

Zechariah 2:8: "For this is what the LORD Almighty says: 'After the Glorious One has sent me against the nations that have plundered you—for whoever touches you touches the apple of his eye . . . '"

Psalm 45:10–11: "Royal bride, listen. Think about this and pay attention to it. Forget about your people and the home you came from." *(NIrV)*

Psalm 45:11: "The king is charmed by your beauty." *(NIrV)*
Psalm 45:11 from *The Message*: "The King is wild for you!"

Chapter 12: I Have . . . A Secure Cornerstone
Scarves of Truth

- You are not alone in your struggle with insecurity.
- We already have all we need to be secure.
- Jesus lived and died to be the cornerstone for humankind.
- Our lives must be built with Jesus as our personal cornerstone.
- When we rely on Jesus as our cornerstone, our personal walls cannot be shaken.
- With Jesus as our cornerstone, God's armor is at our fingertips.
- With Jesus as our cornerstone, we have hope.

Handbag of the Spirit

Isaiah 28:16: "So this is what the Sovereign LORD says: 'See, I lay a stone in Zion, a tested stone, a precious cornerstone for a sure foundation; the one who relies on it will never be stricken with panic.'"

Matthew 21:42 from *New Living Translation*: "Then Jesus asked them, 'Didn't you ever read this in the Scriptures? 'The stone that the builders rejected has now become the cornerstone. This is the LORD's doing, and it is wonderful to see.'"

1 Corinthians 3:10–11: "By the grace God has given me, I laid a foundation as a wise builder, and someone else is building on it. But each one should build with care. For no one can lay any foundation other than the one already laid, which is Jesus Christ."

2 Corinthians 11:25–27: "Three times I was beaten with rods, once I was pelted with stones, three times I was shipwrecked, I spent a night and a day in the open sea, I have been

constantly on the move. I have been in danger from rivers, in danger from bandits, in danger from my fellow Jews, in danger from Gentiles; in danger in the city, in danger in the country, in danger at sea; and in danger from false believers. I have labored and toiled and have often gone without sleep; I have known hunger and thirst and have often gone without food; I have been cold and naked."

2 Corinthians 13:4: "For to be sure, he was crucified in weakness, yet he lives by God's power. Likewise, we are weak in him, yet by God's power we will live with him in our dealing with you."

Ephesians 6:10–18: "Finally, be strong in the Lord and in his mighty power. Put on the full armor of God, so that you can take your stand against the devil's schemes. For our struggle is not against flesh and blood, but against the rulers, against the authorities, against the powers of this dark world and against the spiritual forces of evil in the heavenly realms. Therefore put on the full armor of God, so that when the day of evil comes, you may be able to stand your ground, and after you have done everything, to stand. Stand firm then, with the belt of truth buckled around your waist, with the breastplate of righteousness in place, and with your feet fitted with the readiness that comes from the gospel of peace. In addition to all this, take up the shield of faith, with which you can extinguish all the flaming arrows of the evil one. Take the helmet of salvation and the sword of the Spirit, which is the word of God. And pray in the Spirit on all occasions with all kinds of prayers and requests. With this in mind, be alert and always keep on praying for all the Lord's people."

Hebrews 11:1: "Now faith is confidence in what we hope for and assurance about what we do not see."

Ephesians 2:19–21: "Consequently, you are no longer foreigners and strangers, but fellow citizens with God's people and also members of his household, built on the foundation of the apostles and prophets, with Christ Jesus himself as the chief cornerstone. In him the whole building is joined together and rises to become a holy temple in the Lord."

Sources

CHAPTER 2: IF I ONLY HAD . . . HEALTHY THOUGHTS

1. Meyers, Joyce. *Power Thoughts*. New York: Faith Words, 2010. Page 29.

CHAPTER 3: IF I ONLY HAD . . . PEACE

1. ten Boom, Corrie and Elizabeth and John Sherrill. *The Hiding Place*. Grand Rapids: Chosen Books, 1971. Page 42.

CHAPTER 5: IF I ONLY HAD . . . A BRAIN

1. "Mobile Passes Print in Time-Spent Among US Adults." *eMarketer Digital Intelligence*. December 12, 2011, posted on www.emarketer.com/ PressRelease.aspx?R=1008732 (accessed May 24, 2012).
2. "Zeno of Citium." *Wikiquote*. February 28, 2012. posted on en.wikiquote.org/ wiki/Zeno_of_Citium (accessed May 26, 2012).

CHAPTER 6: IF I ONLY HAD . . . A NORMAL FAMILY

1. Eastman, P.D. *Are You My Mother?* New York: Random House, 1960.
2. *The Twelve Steps:* posted on www.aa.org/pdf/products/p-55_twelvestepsil- lustrated.pdf (accessed on May 30, 2010)

CHAPTER 7: IF I ONLY HAD . . . A BETTER MARRIAGE

1. Doliner, Roy and Rabbi Benjamin Blech. *The Sistine Secrets: Michelangelo's Forbidden Message in the Heart of the Vatican*. Harpen One Publishing. New York, 2008: page 63.
2. Szalavitz, Maia, and Dr. Bruce Perry. *Born for Love: Why Empathy is Essential— and Endangered*. New York: HarperCollins, 2010. Page 51.
3. Peterson, Karen S. "Affairs Rare Despite Rumored Popularity." USA TODAY, December 21, 1998. posted on www.dearpeggy.com/5-media/ announce04.html (accessed May 29, 2012).

4. Shugerman, Lindsay. "Percentage of married couples who cheat." Catalogs. com Info Library. Posted on www.catalogs.com/info/relationships/percent-age-of-married-couples-who-cheat-on-each-ot.html (accessed on May 24, 2012)
5. Stanley, Andy. "Backpack God." As quoted on Scripture and Short Excerpt! February 16, 2012. posted on scriptureandexcerpt.blogspot.com/2012/02/backpack-god.html (accessed on May 29, 2012)

CHAPTER 8 IF I ONLY HAD . . . A CHILD
1. MacArthur, John. *The MacArthur Bible Commentary*. Nashville: Thomas Nelson, Inc., 2005. Page 305

CHAPTER 9: IF I ONLY HAD . . . CLOSER FRIENDSHIPS
1. Glasow, Arnold H. "Arnold H. Glasow Quotes" Brainy Quote. posted on www.brainyquote.com/quotes/authors/a/arnold_h_glasow.html (accessed on May 29, 2012)

CHAPTER 10: IF I ONLY HAD . . . MORE MONEY
1. Jones, Jeffrey M. "Americans Set 'Rich' Threshold at $150,000 in Annual Income." Gallup Ecomony. May, 26, 2012. posted on www.gallup.com/poll/151427/americans-set-rich-threshold-150-000-annual-income.aspx (accessed on May 24, 2012).
2. "One World– Nations Online" posted on www.nationsonline.org/oneworld/ (accessed May 24, 2012).
3. Mays, James L., Ed. *The HarperCollins Bible Commentary*, San Francisco: CA: HarperSanFrancisco, 2000. (Page 1166)
4. Tavernise, Sabrina. "Soaring Poverty Casts Spotlight on 'Lost Decade.' *The New York Times*. September 13, 2011. posted on www.nytimes.com/2011/09/14/us/14census.html?pagewanted=all (accessed on May 24, 2012).
5. "Fact Sheet." Self Storage Association. June 30, 2011. posted on www.selfstorage.org/ssa/Content/NavigationMenu/AboutSSA/FactSheet/default.htm (accessed on May 24, 2012).
6. Kuo, David. "Rick Warren's Second Reformation." posted on www.beliefnet.com/Faiths/Christianity/2005/10/Rick-Warrens-Second-Reformation.aspx?p=2 (accessed on May 24, 2012).
7. "The Gates Foundation: Giving Away a Fortune." *CBSNews.com* October 4,

2010 posted on www.cbsnews.com/2100-18560_162-6915431.html (accessed on May 24, 2012).

CHAPTER 11: IF I ONLY HAD . . . BEAUTY

1. "Beauty At Any Cost: The Consequences of America's Beauty Obsession on Women & Girls" August 2008 posted on www.ywca.org (accessed on May 24, 2012).
2. Marr, Ruby. "Jocelyn Wildenstein Fixes her Face with Plastic Surgery." Make me heal. November 25, 2010. posted on news.makemeheal.com/celebrity-plastic-surgery/jocelyn-wildenstein-plastic-surgery/1391 (accessed on May 24, 2012).
3. Palmer, Martyn. "Interview: Meryl Streep Up Close." *Good Housekeeping.* posted on www.goodhousekeeping.com/family/celebrity-interviews/meryl-streep-interview (accessed on May 24, 2012).
4. Dussault, Sarah. "The Photoshop Effect." Diet.com. July 10, 2009. posted on www.diet.com/dietblogs/read_blog.php?title=The+Photoshop+Effect&blid=10631 (accessed on May 24, 2012).
5. "When Seeing is No Longer Believing." *ABC Good Morning America.* May 29, 2007. posted on abcnews.go.com/GMA/story?id=3217331&page=1#.T8E3OtVulu0 (accessed on May 24, 2012).
6. Oldenburg, Ann. "Jamie Lee Curtis bares the truth." USA TODAY. August 19, 2002. posted on www.usatoday.com/life/2002-08-19-jamie-lee_x.htm# (accessed on May 24, 2012).
7. Gosk, Stephanie. "Touchy subject: U.K. bans Roberts ad over airbrushing." *World Blog from NBC News.* July 27, 2011. posted on worldblog.msnbc.msn.com (accessed May 24, 2012).

CHAPTER 12: I HAVE . . . A SECURE CORNERSTONE

1. Gill, John. (2011) *John Gill's Exposition of the Entire Bible: Book of Matthew* [Kindle version]. Retrieved from Amazon.com.